Flight Lessons 3: Experience

How Eddie Learned to Understand the Lessons of Experience

James Albright

Acknowledgments

Thanks to Chris Manno for over thirty years of trading aviation stories, writing techniques, and for permitting my blatant grand larceny of his artwork without complaint. Thanks also to Chris Parker for all the fact checking, sense of grammar, and style pointers. If he's told me once, he's told me a thousand times to avoid hyperbole. Thanks to yet another Chris, that would be Chris "CJ" Didier for his help with the missile evasion techniques in Chapter 6. And thanks also to fellow Aiea High School Graduate, Dr. David Huntzinger for his help with the article on procedural intentional non-compliance in Chapter 8. Finally, thanks to Steven Foltz for keeping me honest on Gulfstream III systems and procedures. (I've forgotten so much.)

Thank you especially to Grace (*The Lovely Mrs. Haskel*) for proofreading this five times and living through it the first time. I hope this doesn't generate any flash backs.

James' Lawyer Advises:

Always remember that James, when you get right down to it, is just a pilot. He tries to give you the facts from the source materials but maybe he got it wrong, maybe he is out of date. Sure, he warns you when he is giving you his personal techniques, but you should always follow your primary guidance (aircraft manuals, government regulations, etc.) before listening to James.

Contents

Experto Crede

89th Airlift Wing Patch (USAF Drawing)

"Nutcracker fail," I heard from the right seat. I looked down, just forward of the throttles and my right knee. His left index finger was on the test switch, which showed our left system was green and the right system was not. This would be a problem.

Most airplanes need some kind of wizardry to figure out if they are in the air or on the ground and it isn't as easy as looking out of a window. (The answer has to be correct day or night, good weather or bad.) The answer – ground or air – is critical. You certainly wouldn't want to be able to retract the landing gear on the ground; that would ruin your paycheck. But you would be very unhappy if a thrust reverser deployed while in the air; that would ruin your life.

The designers at Gulfstream gave us a switch on each main landing gear that was actuated by two arms that swung open as the aircraft lifted off the ground and swung closed as the aircraft returned to earth. To the designer's eye the two arms looked like a nutcracker and in the Gulfstream III that is what those switches were called: nutcrackers.

Both switches had a vote, but the vote was rigged in favor of being in the air. If either switch decided it was in the air, the aircraft's many systems would conclude they were in the "air mode." (Even if it wasn't.) If both switches agreed that the airplane was on the ground, it was indeed in the "ground mode."

The reason for this paranoia sat on top of the airplane's wings where six panels resided. These panels were called ground spoilers because they popped up into the air stream and spoiled much of the lift produced by the wing, increasing the weight placed on the wheels and the effectiveness of the wheel brakes. You didn't want this happening with the airplane still in the air. The first Gulfstream jet ever lost, a GII, crashed in 1974 because of a malfunction of this very system. Our GIII's nutcracker system was virtually identical to that of the lost jet. We were still at 3,000 feet and those spoilers were an immediate threat.

"Charlie, pull the ground spoiler circuit breaker, behind me, row C, column 9," I said. "Hank, run the nutcracker fail checklist." Flight Engineer Technical Sergeant Charlie Halston reached behind my head to pull the circuit breaker, ending the threat of our Gulfstream's ground spoilers inadvertently deploying and forcing our airplane out of the sky prematurely. Lieutenant Colonel Hank Richards, a fully qualified aircraft commander but sitting in the copilot position, opened his checklist to the page in question. I knew he had the checklist memorized and that our squadron expected us to run it by memory. But we both knew this could be life and death; the checklist exists for a reason.

"Ground spoilers off," he began and then rattled off the rest of the checklist. Hank had twice my Gulfstream experience but clung to the, "Ah shucks" persona favored by many Air Force pilots. I had always thought him to be lax in systems knowledge. "If the nutcracker stays in the air mode you aren't going to have any nose wheel steering, no anti-skid braking, and the landing gear safety solenoid is gone. You may, or may not, have thrust reversers." Perhaps he was sharper than I thought.

I watched as the glide slope pointer centered, double-checked the disabled ground spoiler switch, and pulled the throttles back a full knob-width. "Full flaps," I said. "Well, we've got all eleven thousand feet of runway, but only the middle thirty feet are plowed. The braking action is fair and we've got a ten knot direct crosswind. We are worried about an inadvertent ground spoiler deployment when the throttles hit idle. We are worried about directional control on a snow-covered runway with a crosswind because we don't have nosewheel steering. We are worried about braking without anti-skid. We're worried about the gear collapsing if we hit too hard. Is there anything else we are worried about?"

"That's plenty," Hank said, a slight tremble telling me he wasn't so "ah shucks" anymore.

"Do we have any other options?" I asked, knowing the answer.

"No," he and the flight engineer said together. The forecast was for snow and nothing more. Sometime between our takeoff from Cincinnati and our arrival the entire east coast was shellacked in snow, sleet, and then more snow. Andrews Air Force Base, sitting just eleven miles southeast of the White House, stayed open throughout, managing to keep a narrow strip of runway open for its aircraft arriving from all over the world. We were the last of ten arrivals for the night. Meanwhile, the civilian airports were closing, one-by-one. Just as we began our instrument approach, the last one, Washington National, threw in the towel.

"You got enough fuel for three tries," the flight engineer reported, "but not enough to go anywhere else."

"Before Landing checklist is complete," Hank reported finally. "I'm glad I get to watch this."

"I'm going to put the airplane down gently right on the numbers," I said. "Engineer will get the speed brakes. I will go to idle reverse on the engines, but no more. We'll get a feel for directional control and I'll try to do that with ailerons and rudder only until I can't. Then I'll go for the brakes. The airplane is going to weather vane left. If it looks like I am losing it, Hank, take the engines from me and use right reverser if we got it, left forward thrust if we don't, to keep us on centerline."

"You got it," he said.

"Charlie," I said over the interphone, "we haven't briefed anyone else. If I say the word, you take charge of everything aft and get the passengers out of the airplane, off the runway, and keep them together. How many we got?"

"Eight pax and five crew, sir," he said. "I'll take care of everything behind the cockpit."

"Passing a thousand," Hank said. The altimeter slowly unwound, and I watched as the vertical velocity needle settled on 600 feet per minute, right where I wanted it. The needles were centered and our ground speed was right at 120 knots. I had a decision to make at 100 feet above the runway, this being a Category II instrument landing system approach. The math always came easy to me. My decision would be made in another 900 feet, which would be 900 divided by 600, which equals 1 and a half minutes or 90 seconds. Ten seconds later we would be on the ground.

"A needle width right," Hank said. The math was easy, but keeping the needles centered in the crosswind made things hard. The autopilot wasn't dealing with all the variables as well as the engineers who designed it had hoped. My left thumb moved a half-inch to the red disconnect switch and fired the autopilot from its appointed duty. I dipped the left wing into and out of a gentle bank.

"Everything's centered, Eddie," Hank said. "Five hundred feet and I don't see anything."

Decision in 400 feet; just hold on for another 40 seconds, I told myself.

"Winds 270 at 10," tower offered, perhaps trying to help in the last half-minute. "Ceiling is right at 100 feet and visibility is a half. Braking action fair, reported by a vehicle. Reminder, only the middle 30 feet are plowed."

"One hundred above," Hank said, "still nothing."

That would be ten seconds, I thought. The smallest needle on the altimeter continued its relentless move south.

"Lights!" he said.

I looked up and saw two white lights, then a row of lights, and then the runway. It was still snowing, but the runway centerline lights shone through a few inches of powder. There was clearly a path of less snow in the middle, but the texture on either side was wrong. A foot of snow, maybe. I set the left wheels down first, then the right, and the nosewheel came down on centerline. I felt Charlie's hand slide under my right arm to grab the speed brake handle. I pulled up on the reversers to their locks, waiting to hear the familiar click-click of the safety catches releasing, telling me I had thrust reversers at my disposal. I kept them at idle, not wanting to complicate the directional control problem to come or to obscure my vision from the snow kicking forward. I could see no more than a quarter of the runway.

"One hundred twenty," Hank said, "good reverse." I felt the reassuring thumpa-thumpa-thumpa of the nosewheel hitting the centerline lights of the runway.

"I'm moving five feet to the right," I said, "give me some room when we lose rudder effectiveness."

"Good idea," Hank said. The main landing gear were 14 feet apart. We had a lane of 30 feet. On centerline, the wheels were 8 feet from the snow; moving right 5 feet gave me 3 feet of cushion. The math comes easy. My right leg was slowly extending, coaxing the rudder to the right, which aerodynamically pushed the tail left and kept the airplane going straight despite the wind.

"One ten," Hank said, "VMCA in ten." Our minimum control velocity, VMCA, with aerodynamic controls only was 100 knots. Below that point we couldn't guarantee aircraft control without ground controls. That was normally the nosewheel steering, but that wasn't an option for us. I had to keep in the lane of cleared runway. Having either main landing gear hit the wall of snow would cause it to dig in, pulling the airplane violently to that side. At this speed we would cartwheel for sure. My eyes were right over runway centerline, so the airplane was about 5 feet to the right. The math . . .

"One hundred," Hank said, "starting to move left." My right leg reached the limit of the rudder; there was nothing left. Left. That is the direction the nose started to move. I pushed the top of my right foot to extend and actuate, lightly, the brakes on the right landing gear. Thumpa-thumpa-thumpa.

"Ninety," Hank said, "on centerline."

"You got half the runway behind you," Charlie said.

The brakes would have started all this at ambient temperature, around -5° centigrade. As the friction between each moving disc and each stationary rotor increased, they would heat up and become more effective. Too much pressure and they would lock up. The electronic anti-skid would then kick in. But without the nutcrackers, our anti-skid system was questionable. A locked brake turned the tire into an ice skate. Hold what you got, I thought.

"Moving left," Hank said. No more thumpa-thumpa-thumpa.

The crosswind! The rudder was becoming less effective at keeping us pointed down the runway, but the vertical fin was becoming more effective as a weather vane, trying to point us off the runway. More pressure on the top of my right foot. "Correcting," I said.

"Eighty," Hank said, "almost on centerline." My right leg started to throb from the pressure and I wondered if I had all the pressure the right brakes would take. The limit was 600 psi on a dry surface, but this wasn't dry. I pressed harder, but the nose resumed its drift to the left. I lifted the right reverser handle and pulled up, guessing a few inches would be enough.

"Sixty," Hank said, "starting to run out of runway."

"Three-thousand left," Charlie said.

In the Boeing 747, we would double the distance remaining in thousands of feet and multiply that by ten to compute an on-target braking. Sixty knots was perfect for a dry runway and normal brakes with three thousand feet remaining. The math came easy. We didn't have a dry runway nor normal brakes. I started to flex my left leg muscles and add more right reverse. Thumpa-thumpa-thumpa.

"Forty," Hank said. "Thirty, twenty, ten." I felt the nose bob unceremoniously as we came to a stop. The two landing lights cast their oblong shapes, equidistant either side of the runway centerline lights. The snow, blowing from left to right, obscured the end of the runway, perhaps a thousand feet ahead of us. I knew the Secretary of State, seated thirty feet behind me, might be unhappy with the drama of our arrival and I might have some explaining to do. But we were stopped.

"*Experto Crede*," Hank said.

"Indeed."

That was my last flight as a pilot for the 89th Airlift Wing at Andrews Air Force Base, near Washington, D.C. Experto Crede, "Trust One With Experience." While we pilots were not prone to speaking in Latin, the wing's motto weighed heavily on us because we trained to a very high standard.

In nearly forty years as a pilot, I must say some of the finest pilots I've ever known wore the "Special Air Missions" jacket of the 89th. In fact, a vast majority of the pilots I've known from those days were excellent aviators. But there I also knew some of the worst; pilots that would not have been tolerated either before or since. In the earliest days of the 89th, a Special Air Missions "SAM" flight would append each flight plan with an "F" for a foreign flights. "F" as in "Foxtrot." From those beginnings, SAM Fox was born.

I later learned I was at the 89th during a rare time in its history, a transition period of sorts. This is the story of that rare period. It is a story worth telling because the lessons along the way reinforce lessons learned the hard way, sometimes decades before.

Each chapter starts with my experiences and concludes with a flight lesson I've taken away from it all, updated for today.

Just about everything that follows really happened. I've changed the order here and there and combined a few characters to protect an identity or two. I changed some of the locations to help mask a few true identities. My point here is to tell a story that will help pilots to understand the pros and cons of that mighty tool we call experience. I also make reference to a code word security clearance called "Patriot Blue." There are such code words, but not this one.

Oh yes, one more thing. All the names have been changed, even my own.

1: SAM Fox

C-137C 85-6973 on approach to Dublin, Ireland (Fergal Goodman)

It was not the normal protocol for an Air Force officer reporting for duty. I should have first appeared at the squadron and made my presence known to the squadron commander, Lieutenant Colonel Zachary Marks. From there, I would be given the lay of the land and prepared for the task of getting up to speed on the mission. Instead, I was presented with a letter at the visiting officer's quarters that left me with more questions than answers. "Meet the wing commander in his office at 0900. Do not go to the squadron."

I sat on the sofa in the wing commander's outer office, mindful of his secretary casting a watchful eye on me every few minutes. The door behind her was open, but I had neither seen nor heard anything to betray the colonel's presence. I reread my orders for the tenth time. They clearly stated that I was to report on this date to the 89th Military Airlift Wing to begin duties as a C-20 pilot. The C-20 was a brand new Gulfstream III, the sexiest airplane to ever grace an Air Force base. I knew they would be interested in me flying something larger, based on my big airplane experience, but I wanted that Gulfstream more than anything else in the fleet. What if I had no choice? "How would you like to fly the 707," he would say, "you would be flying the Vice President. How about that?" How could I tell the wing commander the truth? I didn't care *who* I flew; I cared more about *what* I flew.

There was a bang from the outer office and heavy footfalls ahead of the man himself. I had seen Colonel William Edmonds on television many times. Whenever the President of the United States arrived or departed Andrews, the news would show Colonel Edmonds chatting easily with POTUS to and from Air Force One. His ten-second walk across the tarmac made him the most frequently photographed colonel in the Air Force. "Is he here?" he asked his secretary before casting his eyes in my direction. "Major Haskel?"

"Yes, sir," I said, coming to attention.

"Come on in," he said. "We have lots to talk about."

I followed him into his spacious office, lined with presidential pictures and airplanes. I quickly added up the presidents: Truman, Kennedy, Johnson, Nixon, Carter, Reagan, and our current boss, George H. W. Bush. Colonel Edmonds pointed to a chair bordering a coffee table. I took the chair and he sat opposite me.

"Major, when I got the call you were being thrown our way I was pretty upset. But we get a general's favorite pet every now and then and we deal with it. Most of these guys are terrible pilots and it just wastes our training resources to go through the motions only to send them off to some staff job at the Pentagon a year later."

He waited for me to respond, but I kept my silence. I had been out of the cockpit for a year, having spent that time at Air Command and Staff College. Most ACSC graduates go to staff positions, but I managed to connive my way to the apex of the entire big airplane Air Force. I should have guessed at the reception to come.

"But then I looked at your record," he continued. "You are probably going to work out. You see, the Air Force is changing big time. They are going to announce a complete reorganization next week. The Military Airlift Command will become Air Mobility Command. No more MAC, can you believe it? So the 89th Military Airlift Wing becomes the 89th Airlift Wing. The whole shooting match is changing. For the last year, we have been forbidden from interviewing any field grade officers. All we got was one captain after another. You know what *Experto Crede* is, Eddie?"

"Trust one with experience," I said.

"Damned right," he said. "How in the hell am I going to keep a level of experience up around here if I can't hire majors or lieutenant colonels?"

Most Air Force squadrons are built with company grade officers, lieutenants, and captains. The squadrons produce field grade officers, majors and lieutenant colonels, who then move on to staff positions. Field grade officers only return to fill leadership positions. At least that was the theory. Many of our regulations were written with exceptions for the 89th.

"I think the SAM Mafia is going to like you." At last he smiled. If he were on a normal career track, Colonel Edmonds would be in his late forties. In uniform, he looked the part of a military commander. Out of uniform, one would guess he was a particularly fit businessman. His secretary came in with a tray of coffee for us both. I gladly accepted, wanting to prevent my hands from launching into nervous fidgeting.

"Thing is, Eddie, the SAM Mafia doesn't like it when they get a pilot they didn't select. So I got a plan. As it turns out, we have an interview this week with 43 candidates. I had Zach Marks add your name to the list. You will interview just like you didn't have the job. Only Zach is in on this; to everyone else, you are just another candidate. So you lay low today, show up tomorrow for the interview cattle call, and we'll get you hired."

"What if?" I began.

"What if you don't get hired?" he said, finishing my question. "Nonsense. You'll get hired."

He got up, signaling the meeting was over. I got up, saluted, and departed. His secretary handed me a folder with a cover sheet that read, "89th Military Airlift Wing Interview" and had my name with tomorrow's date.

With nothing else to do, I took *The Lovely Mrs. Haskel* and our two children to the Smithsonian Air and Space Museum. The three of them were aviation buffs of the first magnitude and nobody asked why my first day of work at the new job was spent as a tourist in Washington, D.C.

I showed up the next day at the Officer's Club and found a room set up with a podium and 44 seats in the middle, each with a name taped to the back. Most of the seats were already taken, each by a captain. Their eyes followed me as I found the seat in the front row, furthest left. I was the only major.

Behind us we heard a gathering of wing officers, led by Colonel Edmonds. They marched forward and climbed the steps to the stage. The wing commander strode to the podium, tapping the mike twice. "Welcome to the 89th Military Airlift Wing," he said, "the home of SAM Fox, Air Force One, and the finest pilots in the United States Air Force."

He spoke casually about the importance of the mission, the weight of responsibility placed on every SAM pilot, and the visibility of every 89th airplane spread throughout the world. "As you can imagine we are very selective," he said. "I am happy to see we have 44 of you who made the initial screening cut. Congratulations. If history is any guide, we will hire 10 of you." There was a quiet and collective gasp to my right and behind me; 34 of my fellow candidates would be going home empty-handed. "But that's enough from me. Every week we get another example of SAM Fox in action and last week was no exception. Let me have Lieutenant Colonel Chuck Roberts tell you about his arrival from Buenos Aires last Friday."

Colonel Edmonds stepped to one side and Lieutenant Colonel Roberts came to the podium. He was a tall, husky man of six feet and a few inches. His chest was peppered with ribbons, atop which sat command pilot wings. That meant he had been an Air Force pilot for at least 15 years with a minimum of 3,000 hours aloft.

"Hello," he said, "*Experto Crede*, I'm sure you heard by now, is our motto. But there is more to it than that. We have another motto: safety, comfort, reliability. We do everything we can to make it reliable, but we don't sacrifice comfort. We do everything we can to make it comfortable, but we don't sacrifice safety. Safety, comfort, reliability, in that order. So there I was, in command of a C-137C returning from Argentina when we got a number three engine fire light." The "C model," I knew, was a Boeing 707-300 much like the airplanes I flew in a previous life. They had flown for many years as Air Force One and had only recently been replaced by two Boeing 747s. Colonel Roberts said they got the fire light about two hours from landing, shut the engine down, but couldn't be sure the fire was actually out.

"So we arranged to land on the far runway," he continued, "out of view of the press. Of course, we landed a little early so as to still make it to the red carpet on time. We asked the fire department to position their trucks behind a blast fence so nobody could tell anything was wrong. We told them that if they saw flames to tell us, we would stop and they could put the fire out. But if they didn't see flames, they were to wait until we gave them the all clear. Well, that's what happened. There were no flames, SECSTATE got off the airplane into his limo. And after the last press vehicle was off the flight line, the fire department came in, just in case."

"That was nuts," I said to myself, sotto voce.

"That was SAM Fox in action!" Colonel Edmonds said, taking over the microphone again. "So if you men and women think you have what it takes to be a part of SAM Fox, we welcome getting to know you this week!"

With that, the officers on stage got up, we all stood at attention, and they left. A voice in the back of the room announced we candidates were to get on a bus for a tour of each aircraft type. On the bus an 89th pilot, the only one of us wearing the coveted Special Air Missions jacket, announced the plan for the morning. "Each of you are eligible to fly one of five aircraft. We have all five on static display for you with a pilot ready to answer your questions. You can spend as much time as you want, but remember to be back on the bus no later than 1100 for our next event."

The bus wound its way through the base and onto the flight line where we could see a C-12 King Air turboprop, a C-135A Boeing 707, a C-137C Boeing 707, a C-9 Douglas DC-9, and the best looking airplane of the bunch, a C-20 Gulfstream III. Outside the C-20 I saw a face from my past, Major Steve Kowalski.

"I heard you were here," he said as I reached to shake his hand. "Funny how you and I managed to get around the normal hiring process."

"I'm not so sure I got around anything," I said. "I am interviewing, after all."

"Sure you are," he said. "One major and forty or so captains. That's gotta be on the level!"

Steve was hired directly from our Boeing 747 squadron when the White House got their own 747, called the VC-25. The 89th's plan was to put the Air Force One pilot in the left seat and fly the President the very next day. The White House insisted at least one pilot on the airplane be an experienced 747 pilot. And now, even two years later, the VC-25 has never flown without Steve in a pilot's seat.

"Did you hear about Lieutenant Colonel Roberts' engine fire?" I asked. "Anywhere else, he would have been fired."

"This isn't anywhere else," Steve said.

"This place is nuts," I said.

"You keep stating the obvious like that," Steve said, "you aren't going to last long. The regulations are written around the 89th, and the 89th operates around the regulations. You have to adapt or be crushed."

"Safety, comfort, reliability?" I asked.

"Reliability, reliability, reliability," he answered. "If anybody can change this place, Eddie, it's you. But you have to survive first. They kick pilots who can't adapt right out the door."

In the next two days, we candidates heard story after story about SAM Fox in action. The pilots were good, no doubt about it. But they bent rules and regulations to get the job done. Reliability, reliability, reliability.

"What are you going to do?" *The Lovely Mrs. Haskel* asked as I dressed for the final interview. "It looks like your personal ethics are colliding with career."

"I'll do it their way," I said, "until I can't. I figure once I get checked out and establish some credibility within the system, I can change things for the better."

"It's easier to be a revolutionary from within," she said, "than from without."

The final interview was in a poorly lit room with a single chair inside a semicircle of ten others. In each of the outer chairs I recognized squadron commanders, evaluators, and other members of 89th royalty. It was an inquisition; the seating arrangement appeared set up to instill fear in the inquisitee. Most of the questions were easy enough, about weather minimums, aircraft maintenance, and leading a large crew. No problems.

"So far we've given you our standard questions," the lieutenant colonel in the middle seat said. "These are questions we expect the captains to struggle with and you, a major, to ace. And you've done that. But we expect more from someone with your experience. So let me ask you this. You have flown your C-137 halfway around the world to Bombay. The crew has been up for 20 hours, your legal maximum for an augmented crew. The airplane is in good shape and you are headed for the hotel. The Secretary of State's executive assistant cuts your limo off and asks to speak to you. He says they need to be in Moscow in ten hours on a matter of national security. What do you do?"

I knew, without thinking, what I would do. I would call the base and say they need to arrange alternate transportation for SECSTATE; that's what I would do. But I knew that's not what Lieutenant Colonel Roberts did. I remember reading about an 89th C-137 flying from Bombay to Moscow the evening before the first bomb was dropped on Iraq in 1991. The crew set a duty day record for the Air Force, over 30 hours.

"Sir," I said, "I would tell the aide to standby while I discussed this with the flight crew. If I had at least two pilots who felt up to the task, I would accept the mission. I would give the rest of the flight crew priority bunking in the cabin and have them sleep as best they could. When we got to Moscow, I would put the most rested person of each position in the appropriate seat."

"What if none of the navigators felt they could do this?" another lieutenant colonel asked. He was wearing command navigator wings.

"I realize that we can't do this job without a navigator at the top of his or her game, sir," I said. "But between two navigators, even exhausted navigators, I am sure we can get the airplane pointed in the right direction before releasing them to their bunks. It is critical I have at least one nav in top condition for the approach and landing." The lieutenant colonel nodded, approvingly. "The same goes for the flight engineer," I added.

The next day I found out I was hired to fly the C-20 and my Gulfstream III training was scheduled for the next week in Dallas, Texas.

Simuflite is in the business of providing civilian pilots with the necessary training to earn licenses to fly civilian business jets, including the Gulfstream III. After two weeks of classroom, two weeks of simulator training, and a check ride, pilots would theoretically be able to hop in their jets and fly anywhere in the world. The Dallas facility sits just west of Dallas Fort Worth Airport and the Gulfstream III is the queen of the facility.

"Aircraft type?" the receptionist asked.

"Gee three," I said. She raised an eyebrow, looked at my pilot's license, and rifled through a stack of manila folders. She handed me a folder and pointed to the double glass doors to her left. "Through the doors, up the stairs, turn right. Room 213."

The classroom was made for twenty, but only two of the desks had nametags, one with my military rank and name and the other with "Capt. Laddy Costa." Behind the nametag sat the man. He rose as I entered. "Major," he said.

"It's Eddie," I said. "You and I are going to become real life Gulfstream pilots, eh?"

"Yes, sir," he said. We traded bona fides and our paths to the 89th. Laddy was a Strategic Air Command KC-10 instructor pilot from Barksdale Air Force Base in Louisiana. He was a "fast burner," somebody who was going places in SAC. But SAC was no more, having been merged into a new command: Air Combat Command.

A voluminous man entered the room, carrying a stack of manuals, breathing heavily, and sweating from the effort. He waddled to the front of the classroom and chalked his name onto the board: Steve Dawson, Major, USAF Retired.

"Good morning gentlemen," he said, "I am ordinarily employed to train pilots to fly the Gulfstream III, an airplane I know very well having flown for the 89th Military Airlift Wing as a SAM pilot. Now you two are hoping to become SAM pilots, so that's what I am going to do. So if you two agree, we'll dispense with all the civilian protocols and get you ready not only to pass your civilian-rating ride, but also to get you ready for the 89th. Do we have a deal?"

"Of course," we said. Dawson spent most of the first day with one war story after another, all about the prestige of being one of the finest pilots in the United States Air Force. Laddy hung on every syllable, eager to join the club. I couldn't help but wonder how Dawson ever made the cut. So far, every 89th pilot I had ever seen came right out of a recruiting poster: physically fit, clear eyes, neatly pressed uniform. Dawson was not only the fattest 89th pilot I had ever seen, he was the fattest pilot of any kind I had ever seen.

For the next two weeks Dawson covered the systems and procedures required by our civilian syllabus and threw in memory drills he knew would be in our futures at Andrews. Laddy excelled with the systems, but resisted all attempts at checklist memorization.

"What do you do if the ground spoiler warning light illuminates?" Dawson asked during our third day of class, looking at Laddy.

"Ask for the ground spoiler warning light illuminated checklist," Laddy said.

"There isn't any such checklist," Dawson would answer. "Eddie?"

"Ground spoiler switch off," I answered, "ground spoiler circuit breaker pull."

"And where is that circuit breaker, Eddie?" Dawson asked.

"I forgot," I admitted. "It's listed in the ground spoiler failure inflight checklist."

"Not good enough," Dawson said, "you need to memorize the location. Pilot's side, C-9. Not knowing that can kill you."

Laddy erupted. "If it is so damned important, why isn't it a memory item?"

"Because average pilots don't like too many memory items," Dawson said. "You want to be a SAM pilot? You have to be much better than average."

And so it went, on into the simulator phase. Laddy flew the airplane well and his sense of how to extract maximum performance from the airplane's beautiful wing was better than mine. His hands could sense the airplane's complaint when it got too slow; I had to rely on the instruments. But when things went wrong, his performance suffered.

"Fire light, right engine," I reported from the right seat.

"Checklist!" he ordered.

I dutifully raised the checklist while saying softly, "you want me to pull the throttle back or something?"

"Yeah," he yelled, "do it!"

With each passing simulator ride Laddy was slowly coming up to speed, albeit civilian speed. He became comfortable in memorizing only the memory items and calling for the correct checklist when the checklist was called for. I was doing my best to learn the 89th method, memorizing all normal checklists and getting the first three steps of most of the emergency procedures.

"Good job, Eddie," Dawson said after our check ride. "You are going to shoot right up the SAM Fox pyramid. Laddy, you will make a fine civilian Gulfstream pilot. But you are going to have a rough first couple of years at Andrews."

"Pyramid?" Laddy and I asked together.

Dawson explained that military rank meant very little among the SAM Mafia. Air Force One affiliation trumped all. After that, it was crew position that mattered. A copilot was on the very bottom among those qualified. A copilot could not be used on a trip without an instructor and was therefore useless. Even the worst flight engineer, radio operator, or flight attendant carried more weight. "Worm shit," is how Dawson ranked a copilot. Next came aircraft commanders. "You can send two aircraft commanders on the road and that means a set of passengers get to where they want to go." But even aircraft commanders had to genuflect to any instructor pilot. Then came any evaluator pilot and above all else were the crew of Air Force One.

"How does worm shit climb this pyramid?" I asked.

"First, you got to get qualified," Dawson said. "And you aren't getting qualified until you've memorized every normal procedures checklist. You might as well start now." He went on to say that an instructor pilot needed to memorize every checklist, even the emergency procedures. An evaluator had to know the procedures behind the checklists.

"How long does that typically take?" I asked.

"You can get qualified in a month or six months," he said. "If you take much longer they will start looking to get rid of you. Once you do that, it typically takes three to five years to make aircraft commander."

"What?" we both asked.

"That's what it takes," he said. "You don't think we turn just anyone loose with our nation's top leaders in back, do you?"

We both managed to complete the program; though Dawson made it clear Laddy would have some more work to do. It was as if he was trying to prepare Laddy for future disappointments. Laddy and I shared row 14 on a TWA flight back to D.C. and basked in our accomplishment. The simulator was good enough to have the Gulfstream type rating added to our licenses and we were, in a very technical sense, Gulfstream pilots. I couldn't help but think the experience had sapped the bravado of the young captain I had met four weeks earlier.

"You seem like a by-the-book kind of pilot," he finally said. "Are you really going to fly the airplane like Dawson said?"

"I'll try it their way until I make aircraft commander," I said. "There's not much a copilot can do to effect change."

"Yeah," he said, "I guess. But what's the point of having a checklist if you aren't going to use it?"

"I wonder if Dawson was just trying to scare us," I said. "No pilot can be expected to remember hundreds of steps without making a mistake now and then. Some of those mistakes can kill you after all."

"You can have my checklist," Laddy said, "after you pry it from my cold, dead fingers."

"Hopefully it won't come to that," I said.

Checklist Philosophy

A checklist incorporates the collective wisdom and knowledge of the manufacturer, their test pilots, and engineers. It allows you to gain the experiences of those who designed it and those who used it before you without complaint. But it depends on you understanding it and then using it.

Are checklists required?

[14 CFR 91, §91.503 (b)] Each cockpit checklist must contain the following procedures and shall be used by the flight crewmembers when operating the airplane:

(1) Before starting engines.

(2) Before takeoff.

(3) Cruise.

(4) Before landing.

(5) After landing.

(6) Stopping engines.

(7) Emergencies.

Methods of Checklist Accomplishment

The following reference is mandatory for U.S. commercial operators and is considered a "best practice" for everyone else.

[FAA Order 8900.1, Volume 3, Chapter 32, 3-3403]

A. "Challenge-Do-Verify." The CDV method consists of a crewmember making a challenge before an action is initiated, taking the action, and then verifying that the action item has been accomplished. The CDV method is most effective when one crewmember issues the challenge and the second crewmember takes the action and responds to the first crewmember, verifying that the action was taken. This method requires that the checklist be accomplished methodically, one item at a time, in an unvarying sequence.

B. "Do Verify." The DV method (or "clean-up" method) consists of the checklist being accomplished in a variable sequence without a preliminary challenge. After all of the action items on the checklist have been completed, the checklist is then read again while each item is verified. The DV method allows the flightcrew to use flow patterns from memory to accomplish a series of actions quickly and efficiently. Each individual crewmember can work independently, which helps balance the workload between crewmembers.

Selection of Method

[FAA Order 8900.1, Volume 3, Chapter 32, 3-3404 B. 10)] All checklists, except the after-takeoff and after-landing checklists, should be accomplished by one crewmember reading the checklist items and a second crewmember confirming and responding to each item.

It certainly makes sense that the after takeoff and after landing checklists are exceptions, you are very busy and your eyes need to be outside. But every other checklist needs to be accomplished using the CDV method.

[14 CFR 91, Title 14: Aeronautics and Space, General Operating and Flight Rules, Federal Aviation Administration, Department of Transportation]

[FAA Order 8900]

[Items in blue are my comments.]

2: Superman

C-20B departing Naples, Florida (Erick Stamm)

In the four weeks it took me to do one thing, get a Gulfstream III type rating, *The Lovely Mrs. Haskel* had secured us a base house a stone's throw from the base golf course, received our household goods from Atlas Van Lines, enrolled our son into the base kindergarten, and our daughter into the nearest Montessori preschool. Somehow my accomplishment seemed less significant. "I know you are going to be emotionally detached for a while," she said when I got back. "Don't worry about us, you just get that airplane mastered, Eddie."

"How do you know I'm . . ." I started to ask.

"Eddie," she said, "you do this whenever you jump into a new airplane. It's just the way you are. Besides, if it keeps you safe that's the way it should be. You are useless to me and the kids if you die."

"Cleared in hot," my fighter pilot buddies would say. I was turned loose on the squadron with full clearance from home to immerse myself into the airplane. Step one on that road was to make friends with the scheduler.

"Welcome to the world of SAM," Lieutenant Colonel Hank Richards said after I introduced myself. He wore the rank of lieutenant colonel, but the easy smile of a major. He tossed my records into a manila folder unread, and opened a large three-ring binder with a large list of airplanes on the left with the month to come on the top.

"We have orders to fire hose you," he said, "so I got you on your first training sortie Tuesday, the second on Friday, and another two next week. We'll see how that goes before we waste any more pencil lead on you. How's that sound, Eddie?"

"It sounds good," I said. "But what do you mean by fire hose?"

"You ever heard of drinking from a fire hose?" he asked.

"Sure," I said, "it means getting information forced into you faster than you can take it."

"Well," he said, "that's what we're going to do. You and Bill Carson tomorrow, try not to drown."

I met Lieutenant Colonel Bill Carson the next day in the squadron's training center, ready for a two-hour ground training session, followed by a three-hour flight, which would be followed by a two-hour post-flight debrief. He was yet another Air Force recruiting model, cut right out of a flight surgeon's handbook for an ideal physical specimen. He was just under six-feet in height, had a regulation 32-inch waistline and just a hint of gray hair to make the passengers feel safe. His pre-brief was thorough and ground instruction was very good. He seemed to know the airplane from nose to tail and sat silently in the right seat of the pretty blue and white Gulfstream as I got the airplane ready for engine start.

"Keep your eyes forward," he said, "pay no attention to me." He reached behind my head and I heard the distinctive clicking of circuit breakers being pulled. Steve Kowalski warned me about these kinds of shenanigans, but it was still a bit unnerving.

We worked our way through the checklist and at last it was time to start engines. I reached over my head, selected the "Start" mode for the engine and pressed the right engine selector button, just as I had several times in the simulator. The start valve light remained unlit, the engine RPM needle remained resting on its zero percent peg, and for a moment I thought I was back in the simulator.

"No starter valve indication," I said, "it appears to be an electrical problem. Please check the circuit breaker."

"How do you know it's electrical?" Carson asked.

"The valve didn't move," I said, "the starter valve light is out."

"When does that light illuminate?" he asked.

"When the valve opens," I guessed.

"No," he said. "It illuminates when the valve moves greater than six degrees. So it might be a stuck valve. You didn't mention the duct pressure. If you see the pneumatic pressure drop even one PSI, you can bet the valve is trying to open and can't."

Carson explained why the valve would stick, how to detect that, and how to fix it. None of anything he said was in any manual I had ever read or even considered in any of my previous twelve years flying jets. "We need to be able to improvise to keep the mission going, Eddie. That's what SAM Fox is all about."

Carson reset the offending circuit breaker and I managed to get both engines started and to the end of the runway without further incident. For my very first takeoff in a Gulfstream, the airplane leapt off the ground like a spaceship bound for the moon. I kept pulling back to nail the target airspeed and she kept accelerating. Passing 200 feet I felt the aircraft yaw to the left, first a little and then a lot. My right foot instinctively extended to counter the yaw and I glanced inside the cockpit to see Carson had pulled the left throttle to idle. He tapped at the left engine fire handle. "Let's say your left engine is on fire."

"Throttle idle, fuel cock shut, fire handle pull, fire extinguisher discharge," I said rattling off the four memory items. "Run the engine fire/failure inflight checklist, please."

"I lost the checklist," he said. "What are the remaining eleven steps?"

"I don't know," I admitted.

"That's unacceptable," he said.

Carson ran the checklist from memory and explained that I would have to have each step of the most important emergency procedures memorized before passing my initial qualification copilot check ride. The rest of the sortie was a little better; my performance earning a mix of "very nice," "good enough," and "you need to work on that" grades. The aircraft's instruments were a step above anything I had ever flown. But when it came to stick and rudder, the airplane was a disappointment. The flight controls were very heavy and every movement of the ailerons and elevator required more muscle than I was accustomed to.

"You need to lift weights, Eddie," Carson said. "You are a very smooth pilot but I noticed your performance went downhill as you tired. Good job on all the normal procedures, very good, in fact. But not good enough to pass a check ride. Oh, one other thing, Eddie. Stop calling me colonel. Rank means nothing among us pilots."

Bill, as he became known, left the training room for me to ponder my future. I pulled out my trusty notebook and cataloged all that I had learned that day. I wrote about each procedure I should have had memorized but didn't. I penned diagram after diagram of the approaches I flew to airline transport pilot standards, but not quite SAM Fox enough to pass a check ride at the 89th. And then I finished with page after page of SAM Fox procedures that took precedence over regulations and Bill Carson techniques that superseded those very same procedures. After two hours I was done. It was dark outside and the squadron was almost deserted.

"You done good today," Hank Richards said as I peered into the scheduling office. "Bill says you have SAM Fox written all over you."

"That's good to hear," I said. "I got a different impression from the entire experience."

"We like to beat up on new pilots," Hank said.

"When do the beatings stop?" I asked.

"When you take over Air Force One," he said, laughing. "Things get better, Eddie, they really do. But around here the training sorties are always like that. The minute you learn one thing, they start pounding you on something else."

I scanned the entries on Hank's scheduling book and saw my name on Friday's column with another instructor pilot and the characters "S2" circled to the right. I had three days.

"Fun," was all I said to *The Lovely Mrs. Haskel's* inevitable, "How was it?" I ate silently as she herded the kids in and out of the family dinner routine. I left the table to the room set aside for all things aviation. "Daddy's brain will be somewhere else for a while," I heard from downstairs. "He gets like this whenever he moves to a new airplane."

The second training sortie was just like the first, on steroids. The instructor pilot would pull a circuit breaker and a generator would fail, a screen would go blank, or some other item of required equipment would be denied to me.

I managed to have all the procedures memorized but, there was a new level to the SAM Fox way. Of course there was.

I was descending nicely to our minimum descent altitude on an instrument approach to Morristown Municipal Airport, New Jersey. Both engines were operating and I started to feel comfortable when Lieutenant Colonel Marcus Clary pointed to the master caution panel and said, "Let's simulate you now have a left pylon hot light."

It was a stroke of luck; I had memorized that procedure the day before. "Bleed air switches off," I said as he reached over his head and turned both switches off. I thought he said simulate! "Cabin pressure switch to emergency," I continued, "descend as required, and land as soon as possible if indicator remains illuminated." He turned the cabin pressure switch to its emergency position and casually pointed to the flight instruments.

"What altitude are you descending to?" he asked. Altitude? Our altimeter was unwinding itself below the minimum descent altitude. I pulled back on the yoke and added a handful of power. "Always fly the airplane first," he said.

I got us reestablished at our altitude, only 600 feet above the New Jersey terrain, and wondered what the next surprise would be. We still had three miles until our missed approach point. At 140 knots a lot can happen in three miles. From the corner of my eye I noticed Marcus was talking, but I couldn't hear what he was saying. He was having a conversation on another frequency. What was that all about?

"Runway in sight," he said, "you are cleared for a touch and go."

I landed the airplane and kept us on centerline. He reset the flaps and stabilizer trim to their takeoff positions and pushed the throttles forward from underneath my right hand. "Rotate," he said.

I pulled back on the yoke and felt the airplane climb skyward. "Gear up," I commanded, and then, "Flaps up."

Marcus reached cross-cockpit and clipped a new approach plate on my yoke. "Fly us to this intersection," he said, pointing to a waypoint on the new chart.

"What?"

"Just do it," he commanded.

It was a point in space just north of Lehigh Valley Airport in Allentown, Pennsylvania. I had never heard of the airport, but according to the chart it was just south of a VHF Omnidirectional Range (VOR) beacon. The waypoint was further north another six miles. It was a fix-to-fix navigation problem. I had a needle pointing to the beacon and an indicator telling me how far I was from the beacon. From that fix, I had to come up with a heading to direct us to another point in space, a fix. Simple enough. I visualized the problem on my instruments, settled on a solution and turned the airplane northwest to a heading of 330 degrees.

"Come right five degrees," Marcus said. I did so. "This isn't your day, Eddie. Let's say this light here just illuminated."

I looked down to see the "L ALTNTR HT" light capsule. "Venus Two Zero," I heard on the radio, "cleared for the VOR Alpha approach, circle south for runway six."

I spat out the first two steps for a left alternator overheat and somehow remembered to turn inbound to begin the approach as we crossed the initial approach fix. I finished the remaining steps of the procedure and marveled at how I was able to solve a fix-to-fix navigation problem, a six-step procedure to an obscure electrical problem, and fly an instrument approach. Well done, Eddie, I thought.

"You going to fly the approach at this altitude?" Marcus asked. "I thought we were simulating every approach at minimums."

Descend! I forgot to begin our descent to the next altitude. I pulled a handful of throttles and pushed forward on the yoke. I somehow found myself on the Allentown runway for yet another touch and go landing. "Push failure out of your head for now," I reminded myself. "Focus on the task at hand."

The task at hand was more of the same for three more hours. Marcus covered every failure and success in minute detail during the debrief. The many failures were daggers to the heart; the successes were too few and far between to have any healing effect.

"Very nicely done, Eddie," he said finally. "You are just about ready for a check after only two sorties. I think one more to fine tune and you'll be there."

"Really?" I asked. "It felt worse than sortie one to me."

"I was pushing you pretty hard," he said. "You're doing fine."

I spent the weekend memorizing emergency procedures and mentally "chair flying" fix-to-fix navigation problems for every airport within two hours of Andrews. A week later I was sitting in the debrief room with another instructor pilot handing me my third training report with the words, "Recommended for check ride" on the bottom.

"Really?" I asked.

"You'll do fine," he said.

Fine. The word haunted me. Fine was adequate, good enough. Fine was several levels below where I wanted to perform. On each of the three training sorties I had failed to memorize everything that needed to be memorized. I had to be reminded of a heading I had failed to turn to, an altitude I had failed to level at, or a speed limit I had failed to observe. These were basic stick and rudder skills. Fine was not what I wanted to hear.

"Shit hot, Eddie!" Hank Richards said as I tried to sneak through the scheduling office without notice. "Three rides and a check! That's how we used to do it before we got nothing but captains."

The room was filled with captains and each turned to look my way with envy. I didn't feel worthy of anything but pity. I sat across the desk and leaned forward to whisper. "I busted two altitudes today Hank. How can I be ready for a check?"

"Don't worry about it," he said. "They purposely set you up like that. Before every descent point, every heading change, or whenever you have to get the landing gear or flaps, that's when they give you another emergency procedure."

"It's nuts," I said.

"Yeah," he agreed. "But if you can survive a training sortie, real life is a piece of cake."

I spent the next week in the books, only coming up for air on Saturday as *The Lovely Mrs. Haskel* announced it was time for *Number One Son* to lose the training wheels. "How does the bike stay up?" he asked as I removed the wheeled crutches from his bicycle. I thought about that and found, sitting in the shed with all the other bicycles and lawn equipment, another wheel from a tricycle awaiting repair. With a few turns of a wrench I had a wheel without an axle, which I replaced with a long screwdriver and the smallest vice grips in my toolbox.

"This is your first lesson in physics," I said to *Number One Son*. "Grab each end of the screwdriver and hold the wheel in front of you." The wheel was about half the length of his arms and he held the wheel effortlessly. "Now see if you can tilt the wheel to one side and the other."

"Easy," he said as the wheel obeyed the commands of his short, little arms.

"Now I'm going to spin the wheel," I said. "Try to hold the wheel perfectly level, okay?"

He nodded and I gave the wheel a tug and a few pulls to bring it up to speed. "Now try to tilt it."

"Whoa!" he said as he moved his arms and the wheel resisted.

"This is called the conservation of angular momentum," I said. "With the wheel spinning, it doesn't want to tilt. So when you aren't moving on the bicycle it wants to fall. But once the wheel spins, it wants to stay up."

He hopped on his bike, ready for a scene suitable for framing on a Norman Rockwell painting on the front cover of the Saturday Evening Post. Just as a million dads before me with a million-plus sons, I gave *Number One Son* a push on his two-wheeler. Unlike many of those millions of sons, my son took off and never looked back. He rode around our circle for another hour, never once falling or failing to push off on his own. I turned back to the house to see an approving audience.

"One day he will realize just how lucky he is to have such a smart dad," said a smiling *Lovely Mrs. Haskel*.

"One day he will realize," I said, "that his dad is not so smart and is making it all up, one day at a time."

And that only made *The Lovely Mrs. Haskel* smile even more.

"You are way ahead of the game," Hank Richards said as I petitioned the holy scheduler for his papal blessing for the check ride to come. "And because you are ahead," he continued, "you are behind."

Hank explained that I would not be eligible for the check ride until I satisfied all the ground requirements, of which there were many. The first empty checkbox belonged to Wing Current Operations, the guys who do the master schedule for every airplane at the 89th. I found my way to the office and marched up to the center desk. The nameplate read, "Major Stephen Jenkins, Chief, Current

Operations, 89 AW" and behind the plate sat the man. He looked up and read the blue nametag on the breast of my standard issue Air Force blue shirt.

"So you are my competition," he said. "I heard we had a new player in town. You make it an even ten."

Stephen explained that the wing now had ten of us majors in the 1979 year-group and that only four of us would be promoted to lieutenant colonel in about two years. Three of us were Gulfstream pilots, two were Boeing pilots, two were Boeing navigators, and the remaining three were staff officers.

"So I'm the only one with a real job," he said, gesturing to the office, which was his fiefdom. "You being an Air Command and Staff College graduate are a player, of course."

"Of course," I said, leaving out the fact that promotion rates for ACSC graduates was almost one hundred percent.

"But it all hinges on the new wing king," he said. Jenkins read from a letter that only officers with real jobs got. In one week the 89th Military Airlift Wing and 89th Air Base Wing would merge into a single entity, the 89th Airlift Wing. Colonel Edmonds would retire and be replaced by an honest to goodness general officer, Brigadier General Samuel Bullock. Between he and us would be a brand new entity: the 89th Operations Group. "He who gets the most face time with the new general," Stephen added, "gets into the fast lane for promotion."

Our hierarchy in the pecking order established, Stephen went on with the business of telling me what I needed to know and signed the checklist I had to cart around base on my way to earning the right to fly a check ride. In two days I had every box checked and happily presented the completed forms to Hank Richards.

"You are on the board for next Tuesday," he said pointing at the column on his paper spreadsheet. "You are flying with a genuine Air Force One pilot. Kent's a good guy, but he tends to bust more pilots than he passes. You'll do fine."

Fine. There was that word again. I didn't want to do fine; I wanted to excel. And why was a "genuine" Air Force One pilot giving me a check ride? Hank explained that there was only one real Air Force One pilot, the man himself. He had on staff five "associate Air Force One pilots" that normally flew the right seat with him when the President was on board. Lieutenant Colonel Kent Donaldson was the newest associate Air Force One pilot, but had kept his regular job as a Gulfstream evaluator pilot. And his real job on Tuesday was to declare me to be a SAM Fox pilot or just another wanna be.

Lieutenant Colonel Kent Donaldson's only disqualifying characteristic against one day assuming the lofty title of the Air Force One pilot was a budding comb-over hiding an island of scalp poking through the still black waves of shimmering hair. Unlike many of the squadron's lieutenant colonels, Kent looked like a lieutenant colonel.

"Let's get this done," he said as I sat across the pre-brief table. He spread a hydraulic plumbing diagram of the airplane's thrust reverser system on the table and pointed at the two doors attached to the engine's tailpipe. "What keeps these buckets from opening when they should be closed and what keeps them from closing when they should be open?"

The thrust reversers on the Gulfstream III are known as "buckets" because two panels pop up and back to form an almost completely sealed cone to deflect engine exhaust forward. They are different from the "cascade" reversers I grew up with in Boeing aircraft, which at best pointed the thrust slightly forward. With either system, having a reverser come out while in the air could be deadly. The system had to be respected. Fortunately, I studied them to excruciating detail and Kent listened silently as I spoke.

Three diagrams and three monologs later, we were on the airplane and Kent pulled three circuit breakers prior to engine start with the standard, "Keep your eyes forward and pay no attention to me" routine. I solved three engine start problems and we blasted off to three airports for a mixture of three precision and three non-precision approaches, a mixture of all-engine and single-engine approaches, and a fair number of circuit breakers pulled and reset. After two hours my left arm and hand started to ache, but the weight lifting program I had started two weeks prior was starting to pay benefits. Still, I wanted it to end. The fuel gauges told me I was flying my last approach at Wallops Island, Virginia and would soon be headed home. Despite the heavy rain, I spotted the runway and waited for Kent's call to land or go around.

"Land," he said. The wind was howling, but it was straight down the runway. Our limiting crosswind was 30 knots on a dry runway. The Gulfstream published demonstrated maximum was 21 knots, but the 89th decided we could do 30. With a wet runway the charts said 12 knots, but the 89th was silent about our limit. Straight down the runway? No problem; I landed the airplane and felt Kent push the throttles forward for the "go" portion of the touch and go landing.

I rotated the airplane, felt the wheels depart the earth, and saw the altimeter and vertical velocity indicators climb. "Gear up," I commanded.

"Let's say she ain't moving," Kent said, his hand resting on the gear handle.

"Override it," I said. "Turn the ground spoilers off, press and hold the nutcracker test switch. Engineer, pull the ground spoiler circuit breaker. That would be row C and column 9."

Kent's simulated failure of the weight on wheel switches, the ones Gulfstream called nutcrackers because of their scissor-like shape, would send the airplane crashing down if the throttles came to idle while they transmitted "ground mode" indications. The surest way to kill that was to put them into the test mode and then pulling the circuit breaker; that fooled the electrons into thinking the airplane was always in the air. It was the first undocumented procedure I had memorized in the airplane. The procedure wasn't a memory item, but it should have been.

Kent raised the gear handle and reached cross-cockpit and replaced my Wallops Airport approach plate with a familiar diagram of Andrews Air Force Base. "Fly me a fix-to-fix to this point here."

I pushed the thought of the nutcracker out of my head and got busy with my navigation problem. Once that was done we were pointed to Runway 01L at Andrews and I was doing more math in my head. The tower reported the runway was wet and the winds were coming from 040 degrees at 20 knots. A 30 degree crosswind meant the crosswind was actually half of the full value, or 10 knots. Most Air Force pilots took the "30 degrees equals half-the-component" rule of thumb as a matter of faith, not bothering with the "sine of 30 equals point five" trigonometry. Either way, we were just within the charted maximum of 12.

"Gear is down," Kent said over the interphone as I started down the glide path, "flaps are down, nutcracker tests, and you are cleared to land." Then I heard him say to the engineer, "Did we get the F-8 circuit breaker?"

Could he be introducing yet another problem just seconds from landing? What was the F-8 circuit breaker? I pushed the thought out of my mind and swept the cockpit with my eyes to see the three green lights below the landing gear handle, the flap indicator showing the bottom 39 degree position, and that the master caution panel was blank. As I pulled my eyes back to the windscreen, I spotted the first glimmer of runway approach lights only to feel the airplane yaw and sink.

"You've lost the right engine, no sign of fire," Kent said, his hand resting on the right throttle that he had pulled to idle.

"We'll deal with that after landing," I said, "I still have left reverse and plan to use it."

The airplane was pointed right into the wind a good ten degrees and I repeated the mantra known to many pilots, "aileron into the wind, rudder to align with the runway." I gently tapped the left rudder, my reminder about what needed to happen when I flared for the landing. Unlike most Air Force units, the smoothness of the landing was a gradable event and could bust an otherwise flawless performance. With thousands of hours in larger Boeings, I found the Gulfstream easy to land.

The landing flare is almost like a pilot's fingerprints: unique to the individual. Most pilots pull the nose up in an attempt to reduce the airplane's sink rate to zero and try to make that happen just as the wheels kiss the pavement. Some pilots chop the throttles to idle and use both hands on the yoke to eliminate one task to concentrate on the other. That takes a lot of skill; I don't like relying on skill. From my earliest days in the Boeing 747 I settled on what really works for me. I pull back on the elevator with my left hand and try to slow the descent rate, but not stop it. As the airplane descends below an altitude about half of its wingspan, the cushioning effect of the wings over the runway take care of the "kiss the runway" chore. I simultaneously pull back on the throttles with my right hand so as to reach the aft stops just as the wheels touch. There is less skill involved in my method, but it is more repeatable.

As our wheels passed through 20 feet my left hand began the gradual backpressure on the elevator while dipping the right aileron into the wind. My right hand started the slow reduction of engine thrust to idle and my left foot eased the rudder forward, causing the nose to parallel the runway. The main landing gear touched, but the airplane appeared to float. That was a common problem for pilots who aim to zero their descent, but not for my "fly it onto the runway" technique. I pushed the nose forward and felt the struts compress.

"No ground spoilers," the engineer said while reaching under my right arm to pull the speed brake handle. The speedbrakes would extend each of the wing's three panels to half their ground spoiler angle, better than nothing. I pulled the left engine's thrust reverser lever and waited for the "click" of the interlock that prevented it from releasing until the buckets were in position.

"Beep, boop, beep, boop," cried the cockpit speakers. The sound was like a police car in France but the message was clear: the airplane was unhappy. I pushed down on the thrust reverser lever and then felt the stinging pain from Kent's hand slamming on top of mine. I brought the airplane to an unceremonious stop.

"Well, that was fun," I said.

"Thrust reverser," the engineer said.

"This airplane is broken," Kent said. "Let's get to the chocks and hand it over to maintenance. Nice job, Eddie."

I released the brakes and pushed forward on the throttles. When we got to the next taxiway my left hand rotated the nosewheel tiller, but the airplane kept going straight. "No nosewheel steering," I reported. "I'll use differential braking."

"Add it to the list," Kent said.

The airplane was only three years old and it was falling apart. How could that be? Taxiing the airplane without the nosewheel steering wasn't too difficult, even on the rain soaked surface, but I was happy to see our assigned parking position was clear of any nearby obstacles. I shut the engines down and watched Kent sign each of the flight engineer's write-ups. It would take maintenance a week to get the airplane flying again.

We left the cockpit and headed for the blue van waiting for us. Before I left the airplane I remembered my unused sunglasses sitting in their case in a cubbyhole outboard of the pilot's seat. I returned to the cockpit, retrieved my glasses, and spotted the cause of our self-inflicted illnesses: F-8, which was labeled "Nutcracker."

With the F-8 circuit breaker pulled, the nutcracker system would think the airplane was still in the air and that would cause the inoperative ground spoilers, the thrust reverser "beep boop," and the failed nosewheel steering.

"You told me to pull it," the engineer said.

"I told you to check it," Kent said.

After 30 minutes of crossing out maintenance write-ups and an hour of post-brief pilot talk, Kent announced I had passed and annotated my grade report with "very fine performance." That word again. It was starting to bug me.

"That final landing could have gotten pretty ugly," I said after he handed me my official blessing into the SAM Fox brotherhood. "We got lucky."

"You handled it well," he said. "That's why we hired you, after all."

"How often do you find yourself dancing around the edges?" I asked.

"You get used to it," he said.

"But when you pull circuit breakers and compound one emergency procedure on top of another, you . . ." I struggled for the words. "Aren't you playing with fire when you do all that while adding the variable of another pilot's reactions and those of the flight engineer? I thought it was obvious you meant 'make sure the circuit breaker is in' when you told him to check it. And what if I had panicked when we got the reverser warning? As an instructor I've always thought I had to narrow my limits with a student."

"Don't worry about it, Eddie," he said. "We wouldn't have hired you if we didn't think you could handle it."

It was obvious Kent didn't catch the drift of my question. Or perhaps I was being too delicate in my phrasing. I was more worried about his abilities as my instructor than mine as his student. "The Air Force loses a lot of airplanes because pilots become overconfident in their abilities and start to think of themselves as supermen. The Strategic Air Command lost a tanker five or six years ago on a training sortie," I said, giving it another try. "A very good instructor pilot lost control of the airplane after the student exceeded his abilities to recover. Everyone was killed. He was a good pilot but he wasn't Superman."

"Eddie," he said, "you are going to learn that we push every pilot beyond their limits so they can expand their limits. You are well ahead of the curve and as you learn more about SAM Fox you are going to become a better pilot. We are better than that tanker pilot. Our safety record at the 89th is perfect. We've never bent an airplane."

It was hard to argue with that. I let the subject drop and looked forward to my first mission as an 89th Airlift Wing pilot.

Instructor Limitations

A flight instructor's primary reason for being is to allow a student to become proficient without breaking anything or hurting anyone. There are a few cardinal rules that must be observed to keep things safe:

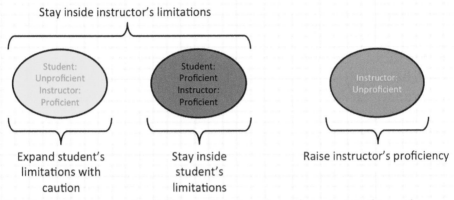

1. The instructor must be fully qualified and proficient. Nothing else can happen until this requirement is met.

2. The instructor must know his or her own limitations and must never exceed these.

3. When the student is brand new, unqualified, or simply unproficient, it may be necessary to challenge the student by expanding his or her own limitations. The instructor must do this carefully, realizing that a mistake could push the operation outside even the instructor's limitations.

4. Once the student is proficient, there is no further reason to expand his or her limitations.

Anticipating trouble

A student may place too much faith in the instructor's ability to rectify any situation gone wrong, so the instructor must anticipate what can go wrong before it does. Before initiating any action that is "out of the ordinary," the instructor must come up with a plan to ensure the mistake will not impact safety of flight or can be quickly corrected. A worst case scenario illustrates this.

An extreme example

In the big airplane Air Force we would practice engine failures after takeoff when 200 feet above the runway. The instructor would bring an outboard engine to idle to test the student's reaction. The instructor had to anticipate a wrong rudder reaction. A common technique would be for the instructor to brace the leg on the opposite side of the engine to be failed as a way of being able to sense the wrong rudder. If failing the left-outboard engine, for example, the instructor would first brace his or her right leg. The correct reaction would be to press the right rudder. If the student pressed the left rudder, the right rudder would move aft and the instructor could, theoretically, counter it with the correct rudder. But even this failed to work if the student was extremely aggressive with the rudder. A good instructor would precede the maneuver with a thorough briefing requiring all rudder inputs to be made gently and only after confirmation of which engine had failed.

With the advent of full motion simulators, few operators would risk a practice engine failure after takeoff in an airplane. But there are still opportunities for instructors to fall behind a student's mistakes in an airplane.

A commonplace example

We are often tasked with supervising a pilot's first ever landing in the airplane after having been blessed with a type rating from a full motion simulator. With enough experience most pilots do just fine. But a pilot without a lot of seasoning in a large aircraft can often be miles behind the airplane, especially with the added factor of winds, other traffic, and perhaps a short runway.

If you are flying an airplane without full controls from the right seat you should probably have the student fly from the right seat so as to give you full control if needed. From the right seat, you may not be able to recover from an improper nosewheel tiller input at high speed from the left seat.

You should also stack the odds in your favor by ensuring these first few landings are on a long, wide runway. Don't assume the student can do this safely without a good, thorough pre-brief. A pilot used to flying a 12,000 lb. King Air, for example, will revert to those procedures when attempting to land a 70,000 lb. Gulfstream without a proper briefing.

Briefings

Before the flight, start with an overall briefing about the objectives of the flight, the anticipated maneuvers, and a safety briefing. For example: "Today we will be flying from Bedford to Portsmouth with the objective of logging three takeoffs and three landings for your initial currency in this airplane. I expect you to fly the airplane in accordance with all limitations and our standard operating procedures. If at anytime you are in doubt as to what the required action is, say so. If at anytime you feel rushed or uncertain, speak up and if you want me to fly the airplane, say 'you have the aircraft.' I will let you know if corrective action is needed and if at anytime I say, 'I have the aircraft,' I expect you to relinquish all flight controls and the power levers and assume pilot monitoring duties."

Before each maneuver include a quick briefing about what is expected and what to do if something goes wrong. For example: "You will be landing the airplane from the left seat using our standard operating procedures. I expect you to keep the airplane on a 3-degree glide path with the autothrottles engaged until they disengage themselves after touchdown. You will fly the airplane with a crab into the crosswind until it is time to flare, at which time you should use rudder to align the aircraft with the runway and ailerons to kill any drift. You should begin your flare at 20 feet and land main gear first in the first 2,000 feet of the runway. Then you should gently lower the nose, pull the thrust reversers to the locks, and then use the thrust reversers fully. You should have the thrust reversers at idle by 70 knots. You should not have to use the brakes until that point with a runway of this length. We should exit the runway at the end. If at any point I believe the landing should be aborted, I will say 'go around' and you should activate the TOGA switch and raise the nose into the command bars. I will ensure the throttles go to 'go around' thrust, let you know when we have a positive rate of climb and raise the gear. If we do land I will let you know if more or less braking is needed."

When things go wrong

We often see instructor mistakes when things go so wrong that the safety of the airplane is compromised. It is important to realize that when the airplane is damaged or when the situation is such that a continued training sortie is no longer possible, the instruction part of the sortie is over and it is time to simply fly the airplane. It is helpful to know a "safe place" for the aircraft in terms of power settings and attitude.

- Power: Go around thrust will almost always serve you well, unless in an extreme nose-low attitude.

- Roll: When in doubt, wings level should be a priority unless the current heading will fly the airplane into an obstacle. This should almost always be done with ailerons only.

- Pitch: When in doubt, climb. You should have an idea of what pitch setting works for a go-around. On most airplanes this works out between 10 and 15 degrees.

- Yaw: If operated quickly, the rudder can get you into an unrecoverable situation. If operated slowly, you might have a bit of adverse yaw but that can be easily addressed a few seconds later.

- Automation: The autopilot and autothrottles can reduce your workload and give you the time needed to sort things out.

Don't forget that the requirement to keep it safe outweighs any training objective. When things go wrong, your priority should be to get the airplane on the ground in one piece with everyone uninjured.

[Items in blue are my comments.]

3: Iniki

Hurricane Iniki, 11 Sept 1992 (NOAA)

It may have been the scheduler's sense of humor or a strange quirk of fate, but my first live trip – one with passengers – was with Lieutenant Colonel Kent Donaldson, the Air Force One pilot that only a week prior proclaimed I was "very fine." It was to be six legs around the United States flying a collection of senators that I recognized instantly from years of nightly devotion to the six o'clock news. As the official copilot, my duties were to coordinate the airport arrangements and the all-important hotel selection. I would get the left seat when he deemed I was ready, and everything I did – everything – would be graded.

The passengers showed up on time and barely paid any attention to the cockpit. The flight attendant had her hands full and came forward every hour just to make sure we were "watered and fed." Kent spent the first three hours pointing at parts of the cockpit and asking for my detailed analysis. "When would that illuminate?" "What would you do?" "Would that mean we have to abort the mission?"

After three hours of that he started asking about Boeing 747 techniques. He had a grand total of 50 hours in the big airplane and wanted to glean any insights from my thousands of hours in the jumbo. The more I talked about the Boeing, the more relaxed he got. The conversation came easily until our top of descent point, TOD.

It is absolutely true that the minutes between TOD and landing are the most risky in any flight, the most taxing on a pilot's skills, and the moments that require the most concentration. An airplane that cruises above 40,000 feet will likely spend 30 minutes or more in this phase of flight. I learned early on in my career that pilots who take these moments in a carefree manner are to be avoided. The rule at the 89th was from this point on, the pilot is completely focused on two things: the block time and smoothness. The latter point comes with experience. The former is a conundrum few pilots had to worry about. But we did.

Plus or minus five seconds! It sounded ridiculous. How are we going to ensure our air stairs touch the red carpet at a time we selected right after takeoff? And how are we going to do that given all the unknown variables: winds, weather, air traffic delays, approach paths, and all the other foibles presented by the gods of aviation?

Kent took two copies of the arrival, approach, and airfield diagram for San Francisco International and handed one to me. He drew an "X" over our expected parking spot and said, "Give me a time for TOD to red carpet, right here."

I measured the distance from the red carpet to the halfway point of our expected landing runway and drew a tick mark every tenth of a minute of longitude (distance) and added 20 seconds (time) to our block time based on an 18 knot taxi speed: seven minutes and 20 seconds. I added a minute for the landing roll out and then the inertial reference system's predicted TOD time. Of course the IRS didn't allow for the airplane's deceleration during descent, so its prediction would be shy. I added 7 minutes just as our rulebook said. I circled the answer and handed my work over to the left seat. The math has always come easy for me.

"You are off by 40 seconds," Kent said. "Remember to add 15 seconds for each 90 degree turn while taxiing and 10 seconds to open the door."

"Yes, sir." I knew that! But knowing doesn't count when you don't remember. I added the times to my charts and busied myself with the many copilot duties to come. Kent hit TOD right on time, I got clearance to descend, and so we did.

Everything was going well, though I thought he was getting a little early on the timing. With more than 70 nautical miles to go, the rule said, add 7 minutes to the IRS. Between 60 and 70, add 6 minutes. At 55 nautical miles, I needed to add 5 minutes. "How's my timing, Eddie?"

"I think you are a minute early," I said, "you need to slow down a bit."

"So were you going to keep that a secret?" He asked. "Your job, in that seat, is to back up my math."

Kent pulled some throttle and let the speed drop 20 knots. As we passed 40 nautical miles I added 3 minutes to the IRS. "On time," I said.

Kent's landing was superb and his braking smoothness was perfect. As he turned off the runway I quickly added the times. "Ten seconds behind," I said. Kent kept his speed up. At the second turn I reported, "On time."

We stopped right at the red carpet, the flight engineer opened the door and as it made its arc to the pavement, Kent counted with the timers on our instrument panels from ten to "three, two, one." My grade report was all praise except for a, "Needs a little work with block times."

Kent repeated his performance the next day and I managed to get the block time prediction to the second. I noticed he flew the initial descent a little fast and passing 60 nautical miles I added the five minutes and came up with the right comment at the right time. "Two minutes early," I said. "Thanks," he said. My grade report said, "Has the block time math down."

As we approached our pretty Gulfstream on the third day Kent asked, "You wanna fly?"

"Sure!" It was to be my first time flying the airplane with passengers and, more importantly, my first flight flying a Gulfstream without one simulated emergency after another. As we approached the runway, the flight attendant leaned over the flight engineer to give her usual status report. "Colonel Donaldson, the cabin is secure, two passengers standing."

I laughed.

"What's so funny?" Kent asked.

"Is the cabin secure?" I asked. "Or are two passengers standing?"

"She just told you," he said. "Just take off smoothly."

So I did. "And you did?" *The Lovely Mrs. Haskel* asked when I gave her the post trip details. I nodded. She smiled and let the subject drop.

I only knew of Lieutenant Colonel Karl Maus by reputation. He was the squadron's high time pilot, with over 10 years in the squadron and over 10,000 hours of total flight time. The normal Air Force limit for a pilot's "time on station" is 3 years with extensions to 4 and 5 years not out of the ordinary. But 10 years? I looked at the schedule and pondered my fate.

Hurricane Iniki, I knew from news reports and a worried phone call to both sets of parents had split the distance between the islands of Kauai and Oahu, leaving parts of both islands devastated. Our families fared no worse than a few trees uprooted and maybe a window or two shattered. But Honolulu International Airport was closed and would remain closed until an 89th Airlift Wing Gulfstream arrived with the state's two senators and two representatives. In front, in the pilots' seats would be Lieutenant Colonel Karl Maus and a brand new Gulfstream pilot who happened to have grown up in Hawaii.

Of course I recognized all four of our passengers as they boarded, but was too busy with my right seat duties to acknowledge their presence. Karl methodically went through our preflight routine and got us pointed to Travis Air Force Base, near San Francisco, for our refueling stop. The passengers wanted their trip kept quiet until arrival, so we picked an Air Force base for our midnight refueling stop.

Karl flew silently from the left seat and left the navigation and radio duties to me. He was a slight man in his middle forties with a thin cover of blond hair. I had never seen him with glasses, but I also never saw him without his ever-present squint. I imagined that if he gave me the chance to fly, I would need to change every adjustment in the seat just to fit. With the seat full up I would hit my head on the panel above.

Karl's approach into Travis was perfect; I was ready to provide the slightest block time advice, but no advice was needed. The passengers asked to visit the base VIP lounge and Karl took off with them. "Get us refueled," he said. "Get the flight plan filed and let me know when we are ready. It is your leg into Hawaii."

I left the flight engineer with instructions with an amount of fuel to upload and rushed off to the base operations office to file our flight plan. The crusty old master sergeant behind the desk pushed the filed flight plan back at me. "Major," he said as if lecturing a teenager, "Honolulu is closed. If you had read the notices to airmen you would know that."

"We are the 89th," I said. "We have a waiver for that. If you don't like it, give me the number for your wing commander and I'll put him in touch with the White House." It was the standard line from our manual designed for this very situation. He looked at me for any sign of weakness. "I'm waiting," I said.

"Suit yourself," he said. "Sir." He signed the flight plan, tore off the first page and handed me the second.

"I need that in the system immediately," I said. He nodded and swiveled his chair to a computer and started typing. I turned on my heels to face two double doors and the sight of the fuel truck leaving our airplane. "Progress!" I said to myself.

I climbed the air stairs and turned right to make sure the flight attendant had all she needed; she did. I reversed course and lowered myself into the left seat, scanned the fuel gauges and pondered how to address the flight engineer's incompetence. We had well over 2,000 pounds more fuel in the right tank than the left; our flight manual limited us to 400 pounds at heavier weights for fear of running out of ailerons to keep the airplane controllable. He had the cross-flow valve open and the left wing boost pumps off, forcing the extra fuel to the low tank.

"I've never seen such a large fuel imbalance," I said. "How long is this going to take to correct?"

"Relax, major," he said. "Pax aren't due back for another 30 minutes, we got plenty of time."

"Pax on the way!" the flight attendant yelled from the galley.

I turned in my seat to see the four passengers walking across the tarmac with Lieutenant Colonel Maus leading the way. I heard the passengers climb the stairs behind me and Karl take his seat to my right. "Close the door," he said to the flight engineer. "Start 'em up" he said to me.

"We need to move some fuel," I said. "We are over the limit."

"What's the limit?" he said.

"Four hundred pounds between tanks at this weight," I said.

"What've we got?" he asked.

49

I looked down at the gauges. The flight engineer was cross-feeding fuel from the right tank to the left and had moved 200 pounds since I arrived. "Two-thousand pounds," I said.

"We'll be fine by the time we get to the runway," he said.

We started both engines and taxied to the runway. "Takeoff briefing?" Karl asked.

"This will be a left seat, rated-thrust takeoff," I said. "I will keep my left hand on the tiller until 80 knots. If anything happens before that, say 'abort' and I will. After 80 knots, if we have a reduction in thrust, directional control, fire on board the aircraft, or any condition that makes the airplane un-flyable, say 'abort' and I will. Beyond that we take it airborne and fly our instrument departure. An emergency return here would be an excellent option. We are at maximum weight, but the runway is dry and long. Engineer, please ensure all four boost pumps are on for takeoff."

"You got it, sir," the engineer said.

"Why are two boost pumps off?" Karl asked.

"Because we are cross-feeding the fuel," I said.

"What's our limit?" he asked.

"Four hundred pounds at this weight," I said.

"What do we got?" he asked.

I looked down at the gauges. "Twelve hundred pounds."

"What are you going to do if we are still above the limit?" he asked.

"Take off," I said.

"Good," he said.

It was a moonless night but bright, white lights outlined the runway. We had the airport to ourselves and tower cleared us for takeoff immediately.

"All boost pumps on," the engineer reported. I looked down to see a 900-pound imbalance. I pushed the throttles forward and felt the engines respond obediently.

"80 knots," Karl said as the airspeed indicator crossed the number.

"My yoke," I said as I moved my left hand from the tiller to the yoke. As we accelerated everything was right out of the Gulfstream textbook.

"Vee one," Karl said as we eclipsed decision speed, the first of several critical speeds. I moved my right hand from the throttles to the yoke. We were now committed to takeoff.

"Rotate," Karl said.

I pulled back on the yoke and the airplane responded without complaint. But the airplane tried to bank right. I corrected with aileron; a lot of aileron.

"Positive rate," Karl said. I checked the instruments.

"Gear up," I said. As we accelerated the need for aileron correction lessened, but did not go away. Passing 10,000 feet I had enough. "Finish the cross-flow, engineer."

By the time we reached our cruising altitude the fuel imbalance was gone and our ailerons streamlined again. Karl returned to his quiet sidekick role again. Most Gulfstream copilots would be consumed with position reports over an HF radio when flying to Hawaii, but we had a radio operator to do that. Any other instructor would use the hours to come for a systems quiz, but Karl was content to sit back and stare at the stars above the horizon. At every position he recorded the total fuel quantity, the time, our altimeter readings, and our inertial navigation system position. Then he would go back into his zombie-like stare of the heavens.

I grabbed a pad of paper and wrote our fuel history before engine start, during takeoff, and during the climb until we were balanced. Karl seemed perfectly happy to violate our fuel balance limitations and I couldn't be sure I got the "what are you going to do if you are above the limit" question right or not. Of course I know I got it wrong from a regulatory standpoint, but how about from a SAM Fox standpoint?

Five hours later we were on final for Runway 08R at Honolulu International. The wind was still howling at a 40 knot direct crosswind, but the rain had stopped and the runway was dry. Gulfstream said the airplane had been demonstrated for takeoff and landing with up to a 21 knot crosswind, but the 89th said we were okay up to 30 knots. What about 40? I landed the airplane.

We had three days off in Hawaii. I took the first day to help my dad with cleaning up the yard and chopping up the remains of a fallen mango tree. I had the next two days with the crew and seeing that Karl could string together more than one sentence at a time. He normally found his stride after the second beer. For breakfast before our return flight he presented me with my grade book, complete with the westward trip's report. "SAM Fox all the way," it said. "Excellent systems knowledge and flying skills. Recommend a recommend ride."

Karl explained that a "recommend ride" was needed before a pilot could be considered for upgrade to aircraft commander, and that you needed to be recommended to have a recommend ride. "You are on track to set an 89th speed record, Eddie."

I was happy to hear that, but still unsure about the SAM Fox nature of taking off with more than double the fuel imbalance limitation. "Don't worry about it," he said. "Engineers pad all those limits by 50 percent. You know that."

"Even if that were true," I said, "a 50 percent margin over 400 pounds puts the actual limit at 600 pounds."

"She flew fine," he said. "Didn't she?"

"Sure," I said. "But how did you know the airplane would do that?" He didn't respond. "What kind of cargo did you fly in the C-141?" I asked, trying a different tack.

"Nothing important," he said. "I once flew with the entire cargo bay filled with toilet paper."

"And if you exceeded fuel balance limitations in the C-141, what would you do?"

"We would wait until we completed the cross-feed," he said.

"So," I said, "flying a load of toilet paper you err on the margin of safety. Flying the entire Hawaii congressional delegation on a trip sure to be the lead story in many newspapers, you take a chance that you can do what you guess the airplane can handle."

"Now you understand SAM Fox," he said, smiling. "You are going to work out fine, Eddie."

Fine. The word no longer stung as it once did.

Limitations Discipline

As pilots we are expected to have a certain level of ego to survive. Without an ego, what sane man or woman would be willing to trust his or her fate to the mechanical and electrical wizardry inside any modern aircraft? Even today's most basic trainer aircraft would defy all logic and common sense to most people before 1903. But left unchecked, this same ego can be a pilot's undoing. Keeping within known limitations requires a level of discipline. Exceeding those limitations is a form of arrogance that must be guarded against. The problem is that many of our peers have the wrong idea behind where these limitations come from.

"Engineers pad all limits by 50%"

Limitations can be padded, but rarely by such a large amount. Consider your maximum speed limitation for a ridiculous example. With a 50% pad, a 0.80 Mach limit would then become 1.20 Mach!

When an engineer does "pad" a limit, it has more to do with mathematical certainty than adding safety factors. Let's say you know a part will fail at 50 lbs. of force, but the gauge used to determine this was graduated in units of 2. So the part failed under test conditions when the gauge read 50 but that could have been as low as 48 or as high as 52. The engineer writes the limit as 50 lbs. +/- 2 lbs. The aviation manual writer interprets this as 48 lbs. So yes, you have a pad, but it is only 4% in this case.

You don't know how much of a "pad," if any, was used. You should therefore treat the limit as just that, the limit.

"We've exceeded this limit before"

The complexities of even the simplest aircraft defy our abilities to consider all the interrelated inputs needed to determine a single limit. It could very well be that on a given day a takeoff weight limitation was easily exceeded without ill effect. But on the very next day in a gusty crosswind, the same weight could cause an unforeseen change to minimum control speeds. You just don't know.

Not all limits are linear. For example, let's say your stall speeds decrease 10% when increasing flap settings from 10 degrees to 20 degrees. Does that mean they decrease another 10% when going from 20 degrees to 30 degrees? No, the change in camber to the wing may not be affected by the same percentage. And even if it was, that doesn't mean the airplane can achieve the same decrease in flying speed.

Not all limits can be extrapolated. There is no requirement for manufacturers to test every possible scenario. For example, if the manufacturer certifies an aircraft to takeoff with only two possible flap settings, there is no requirement to test a takeoff with other flap settings. You cannot assume a zero flap takeoff is possible based on the performance of the airplane with greater flap settings.

"The limits were determined by regulations that didn't consider this airplane"

It is true that many limitations are established by regulatory fiat and the manufacturer must simply achieve the limit required under certification. But under these conditions, you have no idea what the real limit is.

Crosswind limits on a transport category aircraft, for example, are stipulated by 14 CFR 25, paragraph 25.237. "A 90 degree cross component of wind velocity, demonstrated to be safe for takeoff and landing, must be established for dry runways and must be at least 20 knots or 0.2 VSR0, whichever is greater, except that it need not exceed 25 knots."

So let's say your manual has a demonstrated crosswind limit of 27 knots. What kind of pad do you have? You might have a very large one. The aircraft might be capable of 40 knots, but the manufacturer decided 27 was what the launch customer wanted; that was good enough under Part 25, and that's all they would sign up to. Or it could be that the aircraft's actual limit is 27 and just one more knot of wind will be unflyable. You don't know.

"The test pilot said the real limit is _____."

The operative word in the title "test pilot" is the second one, not the first. A test pilot is just a pilot and no matter how many schools he or she attended and no matter how many test flight hours he or she has, he or she is not infallible. Flight tests are conducted under the constraints of time and money and cannot be expected to discover every little quirk of the airplane.

Just because a test pilot, on a given day, was able to extract more performance than a published limit doesn't mean the same can be done on another day. The fact the person making the claim has that "test pilot" title doesn't make his or her claim any less unwise.

The Bottom Line

Perhaps no area of learning from experience can be more harmful than the wrong lessons learned when deviating from limitations without ill effect. Yes, your limitations may have a pad to them. Yes, you may have evidence that under certain conditions a limit has been exceeded without any noticeable impact. But you are operating with a higher degree of uncertainty than the designers intended. The advantage to adhering to published limitations is you know many thousands of flight hours have been flown using the same limits. Once you exceed these limits, you are on your own.

[14 CFR 25, Title 14: Aeronautics and Space, Airworthiness Standards: Transport Category Airplanes, Federal Aviation Administration, Department of Transportation]

[Items in blue are my comments.]

4: TLAR

C-20B in Faro, Portugal (Pedro Aragão)

A week after Hawaii I found myself in Africa and a week after that found myself in South America. The rest of the squadron copilots were wondering what magic I had performed to get such preferential treatment and I was wondering if I was ever going to get some time off.

"You got recommended for a recommend ride," Hank Richards said. "But you can't be recommended until you've done big/small, north/south, so we are playing catch up." He explained that you couldn't upgrade to aircraft commander until you had demonstrated proficiency at a very big international airport and a very small airport, and you had to do that in both the northern and southern hemispheres. And the United States didn't count.

"So now I got that," I said.

"Now you do," he agreed. He spun his green scheduler's calendar 180 degrees and pointed to a line extending from the next day into the next week. "John's a good guy, but he takes some getting used to."

The schedule line listed Lieutenant Colonel John P. Katzenberg as the aircraft commander/instructor pilot, me as the copilot, and three enlisted crewmember names I didn't recognize. It was to be a six-day trip flying the Philippine Army Chief of Staff on a tour of east coast U.S. military bases before depositing him at La Guardia Airport in New York City. I got to work with my copilot duties and then studied the instrument charts for each scheduled airport. Of the six, only the last would be new to me.

"You been to La Guardia before?" I heard from behind me. I turned in my seat to see the man himself. He leaned against the cubicle, disguising his slightly above average height and girth behind the half-high wall between us. His pale-white skin blended seamlessly with pale-white hair to disguise a nearly cue ball head. Lieutenant Colonel Katzenberg extended his hand, which I shook. "I'm John, you must be Eddie."

"Yes, sir," I said.

"No 'sir' crap with me, I'm John," he said. "Eddie I hear good things about you but let's get this out of the way first. I am not going to recommend you for upgrade. No pilot, not even someone everyone says walks on water, can fly to SAM standards with less than three years experience."

"No problem," I said. "I am here to learn."

"And learn you shall," he said, smiling. He handed me six flight plans and I handed him six mission preparation forms. After thirty minutes we combined it all into one folder, which he squirreled away into a leather briefcase straight out of the 1950's.

"I'll fly legs one, two, and three," he said. "If I deem you worthy, you can have legs four, five, and six."

The next day we pointed the airplane south for a short flight to Langley Air Force Base, Virginia, with our ten passengers and crew of five. John flew silently as I talked on the radio and started the math calculations for our arrival. I knew he would be doing the same math in his chrome dome, but I was supposed to back him up.

His timing was perfect, but his approach angle into Langley was too steep. The Gulfstream III likes to descend on a 3 degree glide path, just like any other transport category airplane. I had seen 4 degrees work on one trip and 5 degrees fail during training. We were cleared for a visual approach from 30 miles out and John showed no sign of wanting to start the descent. At 10 miles we were still at 5,000 feet. Instrument procedure math says divide the altitude to lose in hundreds of feet by the distance to go to determine the angle. Since Langley was near sea level the altitude to lose was 50 hundreds of feet. 50 divided by 10 is 5; way too high.

"John you are too steep," I said, "I figure you need a 5 degree descent rate from here. You need to either steepen it here so you can dish it out later, or you . . ."

"I'm okay," he said. "I've heard this about you, Eddie."

He pulled the throttles back a bit and I saw the vertical velocity indicator increase. "You see flying has nothing to do with math," he continued, "it is more about feel. When you get about five years in the jet, you will have the necessary feel. These things take time."

In a few minutes we were back on the 3 degree glide path and a few minutes later John had one of those landings where you had to ask tower, "Are we on the ground yet?" It was that smooth. Oh yes, the stairs hit the red carpet at ETA plus one second.

After we checked into the Holiday Inn I had pre-booked for us and as we stood near the elevator, John announced we would have a crew debrief at the bar. "Where's the bar?" he asked, looking at me.

"I don't know," I said. "I've never been here before."

"Cheesus," he said. "Wait here."

With that he was gone and the rest of us stared at the walls. Or perhaps the enlisted crewmembers were trying to avoid my eyes, sensing I had failed miserably in my copilotly duties.

"Okay," he said, returning from the lobby. "There's a sports bar in the hotel across the street. Let's meet there in 30 minutes."

I showed up in 20 and found the entire crew already assembled. John handed me a Miller Lite and my grade folder. As the crew talked Andrews politics I read that I was deficient in mission planning (hotel selection) and needed to get a better feel for aircraft descent rates. I stole a look at my instructor with my peripheral vision, looking for hints this was some kind of joke. No clue observed; I signed the form and handed the folder back to him. That night I called ahead and was relieved to hear the next hotel not only had a bar, we would be in time for "Dollar Beer Night."

The next day we were pointed west to Fort Smith, Arkansas. Once again the weather was CAVU, ceiling and visibility unlimited, and we were once again cleared for a visual approach early. We were at 10,000 feet with clearance to begin our descent as we saw fit. Once again, the good colonel didn't see fit. Not only was his angle too high, this time he was also early. The Gulfstream III doesn't do steep angles well because of aerodynamic speed limits on the landing gear and flaps. John flew leaning forward in the seat, the yoke barely missing his belly. His face was very close to the instrument panel; perhaps it was intense concentration or maybe slight myopia.

At 25 miles we were still at 10,000 feet, which comes to a 4 degree descent angle. John was easily ten years senior to me, so he should have been the pilot brought up with math. Instead he seemed to be a child of TLAR, "That Looks About Right." But even the staunchest TLAR disciple knew that a good distance to shoot for at 10,000 feet is 40 nautical miles.

It was my duty as his copilot to back up his block time and his descent. But he didn't seem to want any help. What to do? I turned in my seat to see the flight engineer holding the checklist in one hand and a Diet Coke in the other. He wasn't concerned. John taught me he could make it work yesterday. Sometimes a good copilot needs to shut up and observe.

The runway at Fort Smith had several taxiways exiting the runway, giving us lots of flexibility for the block time. He could stop gradually and take a later exit and lose a good 30 seconds or so. But I figured he needed to lose a full minute. If he blew the descent, all timing would go out the window anyway.

At 20 miles we still hadn't started down. "John," I said, "do we need to start down?"

"I warned you once before," he said. "Don't make me warn you again."

At 17 miles he pulled the throttles to idle and pointed the nose to the runway. That came to 6 degrees! And I'd seen 5 degrees fail before. This time it worked perfectly; we made the descent and made our block time.

John was all smiles as I pulled our rental car into the hotel driveway. "Dollar Beer Night!" the crew cheered. My grade report reflected a marked improvement in mission planning, but left unremarked any improvements to my other grievous failings as a SAM pilot.

That night I relived the descent over and over and realized the mistake was mine. At 20 nautical miles we would typically be decelerating from 250 to 200 knots. We had three settings of flaps, each giving a better descent angle than the previous. At 200 knots we could extend the first two notches of flaps, 10 and 20 degrees. But that would be too fast for the final notch, 39 degrees. But that's not what John did. He decelerated all the way to 170 knots, extended the last bit of flaps, and we came out of the sky like a rock. Because we were so much slower the timing issue was solved too. Maybe John's TLAR method was worth learning.

The next day's trip was to Pope Air Force Base, which meant I would be dealing with Air Force controllers, making my life easier because they understood the importance of our SAM aircraft. Pope is in Fayetteville, North Carolina, right next to Fort Bragg. That only mattered because at the southeast end of the airport there laid Restricted Area 5311, what the army called its "High Trajectory Range." I had been into Pope many times and it wasn't a problem. As long as you just avoided the area and the flying ammunition you would be okay.

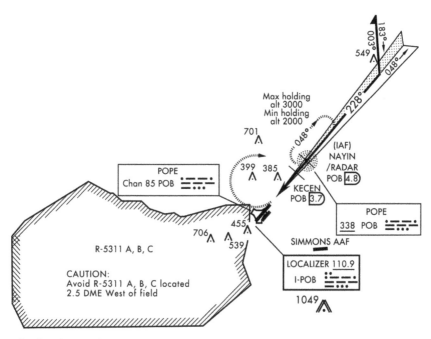

I wasn't thinking about anyone's high trajectory other than our own as John began his third visual descent in three days. We were at 250 knots—too fast for flaps or the landing gear—and 8,000 feet with only 12 miles to go, almost 7 degrees! I had already witnessed him make two descents that I thought impossible. He sat in his seat, his mouth in a half-grin and his right hand casually cradling the bottom of the throttle stems. He wasn't concerned about anything at all.

He finally pulled the throttles to idle and I kept my mouth shut. In another minute we were at 7,000 feet, slowing nicely, but the distance shrunk to only 9 miles. Quick math: 70 divided by 9 is almost 8. Two days ago 5 worked nicely. Yesterday 6 worked, barely. "Sir?" I said tentatively.

"I warned you already," he said, "gimme flaps 10."

I did as requested. Now we could clearly see the airport below us. With only 5 miles to go we were still at 5,000 feet. Ten degrees! We were still too fast for the landing gear; so our biggest drag factor was not an option yet. At the 2 mile point we were still too fast and too high. Now John was doing the same thing I was, straining to see the runway disappear beneath our aircraft's nose.

"Sam Six Oh Two," tower called, "you going to make it?"

"Sir?" I asked again. John said something under his breath I didn't catch.

"Sam Six Oh Two," tower called again, this time with a higher pitch, "the restricted area is hot. Say intentions."

"John?"

More silence. We were now over the runway, falling like a rock, but still about 1,500 feet in the air. Now I could see the restricted area, but we were still at pattern altitude! Ah, I thought to myself, we could do a closed pattern from here! I keyed the mike. "Sam Six Oh Two request midfield closed."

"Hey," the surprised controlled shouted, "that will work! Closed approved!"

John banked sharply to the right and started apologizing, nonstop. Air Force fighters routinely fly closed traffic patterns, labeled as such because they require near aerobatic maneuvers to complete. A 'midfield closed' simply meant we would begin that process from halfway down the runway.

The sharp turn over the runway added some G-force to the wing and helped the speed bleed off nicely. Once on downwind John shot a glance at the airspeed indicator and said, "Gear down please. Eddie, I am so sorry."

On base we got the rest of the flaps and I got another apology. We touched down three minutes late and he apologized some more. We blocked in 59 seconds late and there were more apologies. That night at the bar he kept ordering beers for me and refused my efforts to pay. He peppered me with questions about descent math. "I've got to learn this," he said, "and you have to teach me."

The next three legs were a joy, the most fun I had ever had in my four months as a SAM pilot. John insisted I do my mental math verbally and he dutifully wrote notes with every new concept. Back at Andrews he handed me my grade folder and on the top sheet were the words I publicly dismissed but privately coveted, "Recommend for upgrade to aircraft commander."

Stabilized Approaches

By now, most operators have embraced the idea of requiring a stabilized approach, setting criteria for what constitutes stabilized, and requiring crews to go around when those criteria are exceeded. Typically these are plus or minus a dot on any needle, plus 100 / minus 50 on hard altitudes, plus 10 / minus 0 knots from target speed. Most call for these to be met by 1,000' AGL in the weather and 500' AGL when in visual conditions. All well and good. Except...

If your manual says all that, or something like that, how often do you remember to check your progress? And if you should exceed the parameters "a little," did you go around or did you save it? Well then, what good is the procedure if you don't use it?

And what about all those times you used your superior aviator skills when outside the criteria and everything worked just great? The more times you make it all work out, the more you start to believe your limits are actually greater than those other, mere mortal, pilots. What we need is a stabilized approach procedure that is easier to use, gets us into "the slot" sooner, gives realistic limits, and comes up with an objective way to knock some sense into us when we really need to go around.

Problems

While we haven't always called this requirement the "stabilized approach criteria," we have always recognized that the best odds for successfully getting the aircraft on the ground is to have everything wired and in the slot as soon as possible. But we don't always do that.

Pilot Optimism Bias. We routinely manage to fly our aircraft down to minimums even when things don't go absolutely perfectly. Time after time. The subconscious pilot inside you logs all of those approaches and makes note of the fact you made it all work out, despite the times you were at full scale glide slope deflection, despite the times you had an extra 50 knots, despite the times you didn't quite get to landing flaps until 300 feet above the tarmac. Yes, you are that good. Of course there are countless examples where all of this worked . . . until it didn't.

Criteria Ignored - Unrealistic Numbers. Most stabilized approach policies have a long list of numbers pilots need to observe, each with equal weight and the admonition, "if you don't have this, go around." Most operators preach: "If not within plus 10 knots or minus 0 knots at 500', go around." Nobody does that. Your inner psyche pilot is looking down on all the numbers in your stabilized approach criteria. "I ignore the speed number all the time," your pilot *id* is thinking, "the MDA is open to question too." You are more likely to adhere to stabilized approach criteria if the criteria are realistic.

Criteria Ignored - Misunderstood Numbers. A dot low on glide slope seems pretty harmless but what does it mean for obstacle clearance? Knowing how each of the stabilized approach criteria relate to the threat would help solidify the reasons to go around when needed.

Fatigue Impaired Judgment. At the end of a long day, or series of days, the crew is often the worst judge of their own performances and may not recognize they have exceeded stabilized approach criteria.

Speed

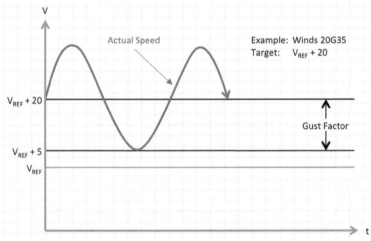

The biggest problem with most stabilized approach rules is that the speed margin is too narrow. With any kind of gust we routinely see our airspeed bounce ten, fifteen, or even twenty knots on final. We need to improve this metric or all the other metrics will be met with similar skepticism.

Most aircraft establish VREF or VREF plus a margin as the minimum speed on approach. It is typically 1.3 VSR but can be as low as 1.23 VSR. Many aircraft use VREF as the correct touchdown speed, though I've flown a few where we were shooting for VREF - 5. We will take at face value that we don't want to ever see less than VREF on final.

We normally fly with an additive above VREF to pad things for wind gusts, short airspeed excursions, and autothrottle tolerances.

So a better stabilized speed criteria could be the Target Speed + Speed Additive, where the speed additive is ½ the steady wind plus the full gust, no lower than 5 and no higher than 20 knots. (A tailwind is not considered as part of the correction, but a tailwind's gust increment is.)

Azimuth

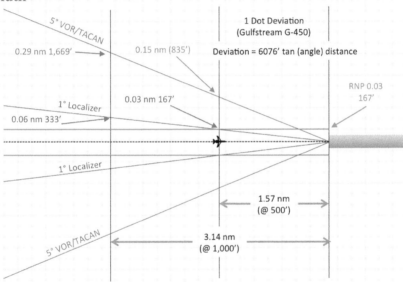

The deviation from centerline equals the tangent of the angle times the distance from the runway. If you are one dot off centerline at 500 feet off the ground, you are going to be 167 feet away from the runway's center. If you are flying a VOR approach it is much worse. Flying an RNAV approach, well, it's better. An airplane with a hybrid GPS quite often has an estimated position uncertainty of 0.01 nm, that's 61 feet.

No matter what is driving the CDI, one dot of azimuth is a big deal.

Glide Path

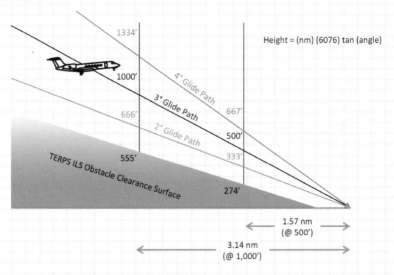

Using a criterion of "one dot" for glide path might not be what you think it means; it really depends on your airplane and the kind of approach. For many airplanes using an ILS glide slope or a computer derived vertical glide path, 1 dot does in fact mean 1 degree. So the closer to the runway you get, the tighter the tolerance is but your margin over obstacles gets smaller too.

A dot for a Vertical Navigation (VNAV) may not be that at all, in fact, it usually means 75' regardless of distance to the runway.

So as was true with azimuth, one dot of glide path is a big deal.

Sink Rate

Most operators define an unacceptable sink rate as anything over 1,000 feet per minute (fpm) though some major airlines will accept something as high as 2,000 fpm. This is, of course, purely subjective. Using the rule of thumb that the sink rate for a 3 degree glide path is equal to one-half the aircraft's approach speed times ten, we see that a ground speed of 130 knots requires a 650 fpm sink rate. The 1,000 fpm sink rate gives us a little less than double the angle and a 2,000 fpm sink rate triple.

I recommend a maximum sink rate of 1,000 fpm and no significant changes indicative of windshear.

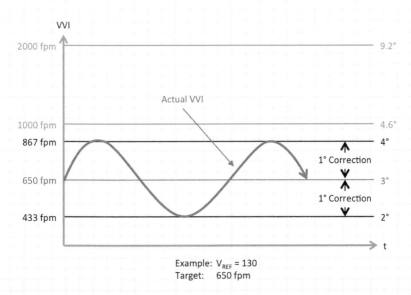

Example: V$_{REF}$ = 130
Target: 650 fpm

Altitudes

The most common criterion for establishing a minimum altitude for the approach to be stabilized is "1,000 feet AGL when IMC, 500 feet AGL when VMC." The problem with this is that there are so many unstated exceptions, such as during a visual or circling approach. The AGL criteria makes the stabilized approach meaningless for some instrument approaches with high minimum descent altitudes.

I recommend using 1,000 feet above minimums on a straight-in approach or 500 feet above the ground on a circling approach or when flying a VFR pattern.

My Recommended Stabilized Approach Method

There is a saying in many amateur sports that applies here: "Perfect practice makes perfect." You need to apply stabilized approach criteria on good weather days as well as bad if you expect your lessons learned from experience to have a lasting impact. Here, then, is my recommended stabilized approach method.

1,000' Above Minimums Check (Straight-in)

If flying a straight-in approach, even if just using the approach as a back up to a visual straight-in, both pilots evaluate the progress of the approach. The

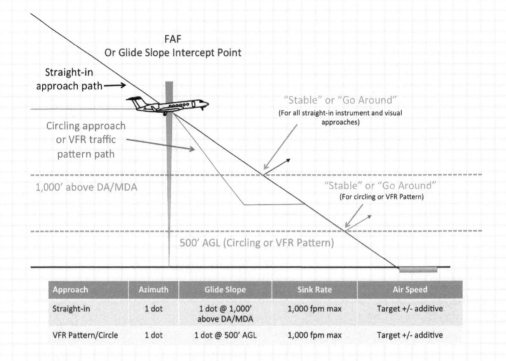

Approach	Azimuth	Glide Slope	Sink Rate	Air Speed
Straight-in	1 dot	1 dot @ 1,000' above DA/MDA	1,000 fpm max	Target +/- additive
VFR Pattern/Circle	1 dot	1 dot @ 500' AGL	1,000 fpm max	Target +/- additive

aircraft should be within a dot azimuth and glide slope, should not exceed 1,000 fpm vertical velocity, and should be at the computed target speed plus or minus any speed additives.

If stable approach criteria are met, either pilot may call "Stable." If the criteria is not met either pilot will call for a go around with the reason. For example, "Sink rate, go around."

500' Above the Runway (VFR Pattern or Circling)

For a VFR pattern or when visually maneuvering on a circling approach, the same rules apply, but measured 500' above the runway. When no electronic guidance is available, the one dot azimuth and glide slope calls becomes subjective. The glide slope evaluation can be approximated using 300' per nautical mile. At 500', you should be around a mile and a half from the touchdown zone. If you are closer, you are too high; if you are further, you are too low.

[Items in blue are my comments.]

5: 12-Pack

GIII cockpit with Eddie's notes (Marc Wolf)

"Haskel, if you're lucky I'll fly your AC check," the voice from behind me said. I was sitting at the scheduler's desk and was happy to see my aircraft commander check ride was on the books for a week from today. My name appeared for the first time at Andrews in the "AC" column, albeit an AC candidate, and to the right was "EP – TBD." My evaluator pilot was to be determined. I turned in my chair to see Lieutenant Colonel Tim Shannon. I knew he was the chief evaluator pilot in the C-20 world, the Supreme Being amongst all Andrews Gulfstream pilots.

"Well let's hope I'm lucky," I said.

"Put me down, Hank," he said to the scheduler.

"So meet me in my office a day before the check with a case of Diet Coke," he said, "and we'll get this done."

"What do you mean 'with a case of Diet Coke?'" I asked.

"Oh I guess you haven't heard," he said. "I am a designated pilot examiner with the FAA. So besides getting your upgrade to aircraft commander, I can give you your airline transport pilot certificate. How about that?"

Of course I already had one of those, but he didn't know that. It was highly unusual for any Air Force pilot to have an ATP while still on active duty. The

ATP cost most pilots a lot of time and money to get, but since the Air Force already sent me to Boeing 747 school with United Airlines I wasn't like most pilots.

"No thanks," I said.

"What do you mean 'no thanks?'" he asked. "I am offering you an ATP! Are you some kind of idiot?"

"You need to do a V1 cut for an ATP," I said. That was the one and only difference between an Air Force aircraft commander check ride and an FAA airline transport rating. The FAA check was usually done in simulator. The V1 cut required failing an engine during takeoff at decision speed, V1. That would be dangerous in an airplane.

"We'll do that," he said.

"That's against Air Force Regulation sixty-dash-one," I said.

"I've been to law school," he said. "Don't be citing regulations to me."

"*Malum in se*," I said.

"What?" His face reddened.

"It is wrong in itself," I said. My high school Latin couldn't hope to compete with a lawyer's, but perhaps my sarcasm would end the argument.

He turned to the scheduler. "Talk some sense into him, Hank."

With that he left the office and Hank just laughed. "Eddie, you have a way of courting disaster. I wonder how you are going to get out of this."

"What am I *in* that I have to get *out* of?" I asked.

"Tim really is a designated examiner and he really does give AC upgrade pilots an ATP for a case of Diet Coke. He wasn't blowing smoke."

"So he's trading a case of Diet Coke," I said, "in exchange for something that costs him nothing while performing an assigned duty on a government airplane. Have I got that right?"

"Yeah," Hank said. "It's a pretty good deal. The cheapest ATP I've seen in the civilian world will run you ten grand."

"This is something that could send an officer to Leavenworth," I said. "I'll pass."

"No you won't," Hank said. "That's what I'm trying to tell you, Eddie. Tim isn't going to pass you unless you fork over a case of Diet Coke."

"This place is nuts," I said. "Is he really a lawyer?"

"I guess he had a two-year delay between college and pilot training," Hank said.

The more I thought about it the funnier it became. Shannon was a lieutenant colonel in the United States Air Force, breaking a long list of regulations for the price of twenty-four Diet Cokes. And he was a lawyer! *Contra bonos mores.* Against good morals.

The next day I was at Operations Group Headquarters, home to our current operations schedulers, training, and standardization/evaluation. I would need an endorsement from the chief of each office before being allowed to take my flight evaluation. I entered current operations to see Major Stephen Jenkins in his element. He sat at his desk with his feet propped up on an open drawer. Two captains stood opposite him, both standing perfectly erect.

"Tell the White House they can have the Boeing 707 for the Vice President this one time," he said while pointing his index finger to the large Plexiglas scheduling board across the room, "but only because the airplane is available. We can't guarantee it in the future." So ordered, the captains scurried off and I took their place, choosing to sit instead of the stand at attention bit.

"Eddie!" he said. "Welcome to my kingdom. I heard you were going to set the land speed record for AC upgrade."

"What do you mean 'were,' as in no longer?" I asked.

"Precisely," he said. "Tim ain't going to pass you without a case of Diet Coke."

"Can this wing really be that corrupt?" I asked.

"Where else are you going to get an ATP for that price?" he asked.

"The price is too high," I said.

"Well maybe I was wrong," he said. "When I heard you were top graduate at Air Command and Staff College I was convinced you had the next promotion in the bag, so that meant one less for the rest of us. But maybe you are too stupid to be a lieutenant colonel."

"Maybe," I said. "But I need your signature."

He took the form, added his signature to the form, and smiled. "Maybe they won't promote you if you don't upgrade to AC. Things are looking up."

"Good news for you," I said. I got up and left his office. I crossed the hall to the dreaded Standardization and Evaluation Branch, known officially as

Stan/Eval but forever Stan/Evil to me from my days doing the same job many years ago. But I was a Stan/Evil pilot as a captain in an office of four pilots, two navigators, and ten enlisted crewmembers. At the 89th, there were 30 evaluators and many of them were lieutenant colonels.

I entered the cavernous office and spotted the telltale signs of a fiefdom. There was only one enclosed space, at the end, where the king himself resided. The 89th's emblem hung from the door and under that was the king's name and title: Lieutenant Colonel Charles Roberts, Chief, Standardization and Evaluation. A ring of desks radiated from this center office, the more important were closer to the king. In the inner orbit I could see the Chief, C-137 Stan/Eval, the Chief, C-135 Stan/Eval, the Chief, C-20 Stan/Eval, and the Chief, C-9 Stan/Eval. As the orbits got further away, the *gravitas* of the desk got weaker. I could see Shannon's name at the C-20 desk, but he wasn't there. In fact, none of the pilot desks were occupied. With each passing arc came another genre of evaluator: navigators, flight engineers, radio operators, and flight attendants.

In the outer orbit I found the office secretary and presented my form for signature. She got up and led me to the center office.

I had never met him, but heard Lieutenant Colonel Roberts speak at my interview and caught war story after war story of his SAM Fox exploits at the bar. He had been a SAM Fox legend for nearly ten years and plebes like me would never get a chance to meet such royalty without an invitation.

"Eddie," he said as he rose from behind his desk, "I've heard good things. Anyone who can teach the Katz a little humility is okay in my book." Colonel Roberts had one of those easy smiles that seemed living proof of the theory it takes fewer muscles to smile than to frown. He explained that he and Katzenberg were classmates at the Air Force Academy and chased each other around the Air Force from one assignment to the next. "Katz has always hated numbers and I could never convince him that there is a better way than 'guess and hope.' Now all he talks about is the math behind flying. One day you'll have to teach me."

"I can do that, sir."

"I'm Chuck," he said, "and we are friends."

My new friend signed my paperwork and I managed to escape Stan/Evil without being spotted by any of the Gulfstream evaluators. I made my way to the training office for my last signature. Major Steve Kowalski, one of several training officers, signed my form as "acting chief of training."

"How did you get around Shannon and the Diet Coke black mail?" I asked.

"I had the good sense to upgrade while he was on vacation," Steve said. "If you think he's bluffing about busting you, well, he's not. I've seen him do worse."

"Worse than a bust without cause?" I asked.

"You ever bust a check ride?" Steve asked.

"No."

"Well then," he said, "you are red meat for the 'humbling bust.' They say no matter how good you are, you can't be up to SAM Fox standards. They'll bust you just to humble you."

"To think I volunteered for this mad house," I said. "Maybe I'm due a bust."

"That's the spirit!" he said.

"Figures my first bust would be from a lawyer."

Steve laughed. "He's not a lawyer. He tells everyone he went to law school and he did. But he flunked out his first semester."

Circumventio Veritas. Truth defrauded.

"How do you know that?" I asked.

Steve pointed to a big filing cabinet. "This is the training office, we've got everyone's training records, including yours, Purdue boy."

I walked out the Operations Group Headquarters just as Lieutenant Colonel Shannon was walking in. Damn the luck.

"Major Haskel," he said. "I heard you have two young kids and live on base."

"Yes, sir."

"Well I guess a case of Diet Coke is pretty expensive these days," he said. "Let's make it a twelve-pack and call it good."

"Sir," I said, "I'll buy you one Diet Coke if you are thirsty. I'll even buy you two. But I'm not giving you a thing as the price of passing a check ride. If you want to be illegal, unethical, or immoral, you can do that without my help."

Shannon just stared at me. *Debilito silentium.* Injured silence. He didn't say anything so I turned around and left.

The next day at the squadron I headed directly to the scheduler's office where the Gulfstream desk was empty. I sat behind the desk and opened the scheduling book and was happy to see my name still on the books and with another evaluator pilot assigned, Lieutenant Colonel Donald Newsome.

"Donnie's gonna eat you alive," I heard from across the desk. Hank Richards waited as I vacated his seat and relinquished the tools of his trade. He sat back with the book on his lap and scribbled for a minute or two. When he was done he looked up, "You still here?"

"I was hoping for a few clues," I said. "If one is going to get eaten alive, one needs some kind of idea on how the meal is to be served."

"Well you never heard this from me," he said, whispering. "Donnie's got orders to give you a humbling bust. Eddie, I thought the way we were fast tracking you the SAM Mafia wanted to make an example of you. A positive example. Now I think they've changed their minds. Too bad."

The next day I sat in Gulfstream mission planning room number one, seated across from Lieutenant Colonel Donald Newsome and looking at a diagram of the airplane's flight control system. The oral exam was going well. After an hour and thirty minutes he hadn't asked me anything I didn't know.

"One last question, Eddie," he said at last. "Let's say you are on alert here at Andrews and you get launched to Europe with a stop at Gander, Newfoundland. The weather there is a half mile visibility in heavy snow, the temperature is minus five centigrade, and you've got a pretty stiff crosswind. But being the great SAM Fox pilot you are, you manage to land right on time. You get the airplane refueled and manage to get everyone on board and the engines started. As you taxi out you ask your copilot to set Flaps 20. He moves the flap handle, but the flaps stop moving at seven degrees. What's the problem and what will you do?"

The Gulfstream III's horizontal stabilizer has two positions and is controlled by a mechanical linkage with the flaps. As the flaps move through 7 ½ degrees the stabilizer is moved to the takeoff position if the flaps are extending, or cruise position if they are retracting. The system is purely mechanical, but can be a problem if the horizontal stabilizer is somehow frozen in position.

"It looks like we have some compacted snow or ice on the horizontal stab," I said. "I would taxi back and have the tail deiced."

"What about your block time?" he asked.

"It shouldn't take more than 15 minutes," I said. "Besides, there are no other alternatives."

"Well I suppose you might do that," he said. "But that's not what I did when this exact thing happened to me last winter. Do you know the average distance penalty for taking off with Flaps 10 instead of Flaps 20?"

"On average," I said, "seven hundred feet."

"That's right," he said. He smiled broadly, for the first time of the day. "So if going from Flaps 20 to Flaps 10 costs me seven hundred feet, going from Flaps 10 to Flaps 7 has to be less than that."

I laughed, which reversed his newly acquired grin. "What's so funny?"

"First of all, the relationship of flap angle to runway distance required isn't linear," I said. He looked at me incredulously. "Secondly, you cannot extrapolate the data. You have no evidence the aircraft can safely takeoff in that situation."

"Yes I do," he said. "We did it. How's that for evidence."

"Even if you did," I said, "with the tail iced like that you should have had trim issues until the ice sublimated."

"Yes!" he said. "We did! And we had to push forward on the elevator for almost an hour until the ice was gone. How's that for SAM Fox in action!"

"I think that might be the dumbest thing in aviation I've ever heard," I said.

"I think you are forgetting something," he said. "This is your check ride and you have to pass this oral to get to the airplane."

"Your call," I said.

I didn't start the oral with this kind of "in-your-face" aggression in mind, but something about his Flaps 7 takeoff struck a nerve. Whenever that nerve got struck, I knew, I tended to get subtly sarcastic and poker faced. Don't betray any emotion. That will piss him off even more.

"Let's go flying," he said.

Engine start, taxi out, and the initial takeoff were no different than any training sortie, including a simulated engine failure right after takeoff. As soon as we cleared the Andrews traffic pattern he reached cross-cockpit and placed an approach plate in front of me. "Fly me a fix-to-fix here then the procedure turn."

I looked down to see the VOR DME approach to Runway 8 and Lancaster, Pennsylvania. The fix was just west of the Lancaster VOR. I dialed in the frequency, looked at the compass card, and computed a heading. Ten minutes later we were on the ground. A minute after that, in the air again and headed to another navigation point for another fix-to-fix problem. As I was computing the new heading Newsome pointed to the engine fire handle on his side. "You've got a simulated fire in the right engine."

I came up with the heading, spun that into the instruments, and dipped the left wing to start the turn. "Throttle idle," I commanded, "fuel cock shutoff, fire handle pull, time for 30 seconds please." As I was speaking we reached our heading and I leveled the wings. With the right engine at idle I remembered to increase thrust on the left engine while slightly extending my left leg to add left rudder. After spouting off the remaining emergency procedure items I asked for the next notch of flaps and busied myself with the approach.

"Let's say there is smoke pouring out of the air conditioning duct," he said.

And so it went. For nearly three hours we flew one fix-to-fix after another, one single-engine approach after another. With every approach there were one or two additional emergency procedures. Most of these were simulated, of course. But for added realism he tripped generators, depressurized the airplane, and pulled circuit breakers to the avionics. We did four approaches at Lancaster, five at Dover, and by the time we got to our first approach at Philipsburg, Pennsylvania, I was exhausted. I began each approach with a manila folder clipped to the glare shield in front of me, obscuring my vision. When we got to minimums, Newsome would either pull the manila folder away or he wouldn't. If he pulled it I would land, and then he would reset the flaps, push the throttles forward, and say, "rotate" when we got flying speed. If he left the folder in place, he would wait silently for me to announce we were at our decision height and initiate a missed approach. From my peripheral vision and every time we took off I could see the manila folder may have been overkill. The cloud deck was getting lower with every approach.

"Missed approach," I said, "Flaps 20, set climb thrust, gear up." Newsome reset the flaps, adjusted one of the throttles to climb thrust while leaving the simulated failed engine at idle, and retracted the landing gear. He reached over to pull my approach plate and replaced it with another.

"Fly me a fix-to-fix here," he said.

"Geez," I said.

"You got a problem, major?"

"The weather has been crummy all day," I said. "I'd love to do this for another three hours, but I'm wondering about the fuel."

"I'll worry about the fuel," he said, "you worry about flying the non-directional beacon approach to runway 16."

The standard SAM Fox check ride "gotcha" was to simulate a failure just seconds prior to some kind of action point on the approach, an attempt to get the pilot to forget the action point. I set up the correct heading to the next navigation fix and would have to remember to make a turn outbound from the fix. With a mile to go Newsome pointed to our master caution panel, a bank of red and amber lights, each wired to a critical component somewhere on the jet. He pointed to the second row, third column light.

"You have a left pylon hot."

"Bleed air switches off," I said while turning to the outbound heading. "Cabin pressure switch can stay where it is, declare an emergency."

I hit the stopwatch on my instrument panel and checked the approach plate. "Dial in the final approach fix altitude."

He did as requested and with five seconds before my turn he pointed to the ninth row, first column. "You got a combined hydraulic light."

I rattled off the procedure while turning inbound and asked for the next notch of flaps. *Another look at the approach plate.* Don't forget to descend, I reminded myself.

The NDB needle would waver as we got close, I knew. I hit my stopwatch on the turn inbound and if the winds were kind, I could guess within a few seconds when it was time to descend. The cloud deck on the previous approach was pretty close to minimums, and that was a VOR approach. Minimums for this NDB approach would be higher. Don't forget to descend. I forced my eyes away from my pilot's flight display just to recheck our minimum descent altitude. No sense starting a descent if you don't remember how low to go!

My eyes darted back to my pilot's flight display in time to see it flicker off. I glanced to my right only to see that his were off as well. Standby instruments next. They were working. There goes the NDB needle. Time to descend. I pulled the left throttle back the width of the knob and relaxed pressure on the left rudder.

As we descended through 2,000 feet I double-checked my situation, just to be sure. I had the right engine at idle, simulated failed. The left pylon was simulated overheated and both bleed switches were off; our airplane was completely depressurized as a result. The hydraulic system was simulated failed as well, but Newsome hadn't pulled any circuit breakers or turned off anything related. *As far as I knew.* Oh yes, the only flight instrument I had left was an emergency back up gauge. And we were in the weather. All things considered, I had handled it all pretty well. Why is it so quiet?

Another scan. The landing gear is still up! I was supposed to get that before we started our descent from the final approach fix. "Gear down," I barked, "before landing checklist, please."

The gear cycled down with its reassuring thud and each light assigned to each landing leg illuminated bright green. I realized that for the first time that day I had raised my voice, betraying emotion and my failure. But I somehow remembered to level off at the minimum descent altitude and to execute the missed approach when our timing expired. I flew silently as Newsome and the flight engineer exchanged expletives trying to restore the flight instruments. Our cathode ray tubes were refusing to return to life after having their circuit breakers pulled. By the time we showed up at Andrews, half the electrons were happy again and half the tubes came back. I landed. As the engines spooled down I scanned my notepad. It was 12 approaches, all of them single-engine. It was a 12-pack.

"So how do you think you did?" Newsome asked while we sat on opposite sides of his desk in the bowels of Stan/Evil.

"Very well," I said.

"You fly a pretty good airplane, Eddie," he said. "But you aren't perfect." Newsome detailed the first ten approaches and the twelfth. Navigation was "exceptional." Emergency procedures were "extremely fine." Landings were "great." He waxed poetic and was my biggest fan for about 30 minutes. He smiled broadly throughout and it appeared to me he was ready to sign up for my fan club. "But that last approach at Phillipsburg is a problem," he said. The "U" of his broad smile turned into the hyphen of a gravely serious pout. "Let me ask you one last question. When does the regulation say the landing gear has to be down on an instrument approach?"

Ah, that was it. By Air Force regulation, the landing gear had to be down before the final approach fix or glide slope intercept on an instrument approach. An *instrument* approach. That word set my tongue forward on one of its calmly spoken but uncensored soliloquys. "Your tongue is like a sword," my mom used to say. *Let the skewering begin.*

"I'll answer your question," I said, "but you have to answer twelve of mine. "By regulation, how high must you be to pull an engine for a simulated failure? I saw 100 feet today; the regulation says 200. By regulation, can you have an engine pulled back in the weather? The book says no; today all 12 approaches were in the weather and all 12 had an engine pulled back." Newsome's hyphen turned into an unhappy backslash. "By regulation," I continued, "are you allowed to trip the primary display circuit breakers while in flight on any day, much less a day in instrument conditions? No, by regulation . . ."

"That's enough, major," he said, rising. "This is the 89th and I will be damned if I sit here and let you lecture me about regulations. Let's just hope your recheck goes better."

Newsome walked the length of the room to Tim Shannon's desk and the two huddled in not quite a whisper but not quite loud enough for me to decipher the unfolding strategy. I hadn't expected any of this. I retrieved the kneeboard notes I kept and pulled out a clean sheet of paper to add details. For the first time ever I started to look at these notes of mine as legal documents. *Evidentia vindico.* Preserve the evidence. I drew twelve diagrams with arrows to the point of each simulated or real failure.

"It's clearly a bustable offense!" I heard from across the room. The two composed themselves and got up. Bisecting a line between Shannon's desk and Newsome's, there was an aisle to the king's office. Shannon rapped his knuckles against the door and the two entered Lieutenant Colonel Chuck Roberts' office and closed the door behind them.

The muffled voices were clearly from Newsome and Shannon. *Prosequi a fortiori.* The prosecution pleads. Then there was another voice. It had to be Roberts. *Amicus curiae.* A friend of the court. The door opened and Shannon stormed out, red faced. Newsome walked meekly to a word processor and typed. A machine whirred into action and spat out my check ride results. Newsome retrieved the form, signed, and returned to his desk. "Sign here," he said. I took the form and read the word "QUALIFIED" and signed. I looked at Newsome who diverted his eyes.

I left the office, a newly upgraded SAM Fox aircraft commander.

Humility

A common thread that weaves through many aircraft mishaps is what appears to be pure stupidity ("Why would anyone do that?") or ignorance ("Why didn't they know better?"). You can also detect a similar tendency among peers you would like to avoid ("Doesn't that pilot understand how risky that behavior is?"). The answer to all three questions might lie with a common trait among experienced pilots: arrogance.

Arrogance : noun, offensive display of superiority or self-importance; overbearing pride.

Arrogance is a part of pilot psychology that we don't bother examining, apart from military combat units where it could be rightfully thought of as a survival tool. We are more likely to consider complacency and overconfidence as the root cause of some of these pilot behaviors; but don't these just boil down to a pilot thinking he or she knows it all? When a pilot deviates from standard operating procedures, ignores common practice, refuses to listen to the inputs of fellow crewmembers; that pilot is showing all the telltale signs of arrogance. We can look for a cure by thinking of what is required by the opposite trait: humility.

Humility : noun, the quality or condition of being humble; modest opinion or estimate of one's own importance, rank, etc.

Humble pilots realize that no matter how experienced, well trained, and naturally gifted they are, they can still make mistakes and that they still have much to learn. A humble pilot never assumes total knowledge, relies on Standard Operating Procedures (SOPs), and is willing to listen to the crew. In short, a humble pilot is a safe pilot.

If we examine components of a pilot's character against this spectrum of arrogance versus humility, we can learn how to adapt our behavior and become safer pilots.

A Results-Oriented Nature

A key element of survival for all humans is the ability to tie cause with effect. Pilots must have this results-oriented nature to fully understand the "why" of aviation.

An arrogant pilot understands there are good flights and bad flights, but assumes all of his or her actions will end up in a good flight. Bad flights are the result of someone else's actions, the "system," or simply "just how it goes."

A humble pilot understands that all pilot procedures and techniques are aimed at the successful outcome of the flight. Procedures and techniques that don't contribute to that goal must be examined and improved upon. This results-oriented nature requires the pilot to be honest with him or herself.

A Truthful Nature

The key difference between arrogance and humility is the quality of honesty. Pilots must be truthful with themselves and with others to avoid falling into complacency.

An arrogant pilot tends to ignore SOPs that require additional effort, harm their personal view as "above all that," or require they admit they had been doing it wrong in the past.

Humble pilots realize they cannot know everything, can forget the things that they once knew, and are not immune to making mistakes. Moreover, a humble pilot understands the cause-and-effect chain in pilot procedures and realizes that the pilot is almost always responsible for the cause.

A Self-Critical Nature

You cannot fix something that you don't know is broken. If the thing that is broken lies within one's self, naturally the fix has to come from within.

An arrogant pilot makes excuses for mistakes or finds someone or something to take the blame.

A humble pilot has an open mind when it comes to the cause and effect of what goes on in the cockpit. When something does not go as planned, a humble pilot places his or her own actions at the top of the suspect list, openly accepts ownership of the blame, and attempts to learn from the episode. Pilots who are self-critical tend to operate according to SOPs and have cockpits with less drama than those who don't. Moreover, these pilots earn reputations for drama-free cockpits and the ability to work well and get along well with other crewmembers. People learn to rely on them. In short, they will have become trustworthy.

A Trustworthy Nature

It is easier to place one's trust in someone who is more predictable in each of these characteristics; it is easier to rely on familiarity than capriciousness.

An arrogant pilot follows SOPs only if they think they are convenient or when being watched by someone they fear (a check airman, their boss, or perhaps a safety auditor).

A humble pilot, on the other hand, realizes that SOPs were designed to accommodate all pilots, including very good pilots who may have been compromised by fatigue or occasional forgetfulness. The humble pilot is far less likely to make a preventable mistake.

Trustworthy pilots consistently follow SOPs. If an occasional deviation is required by the situation, a trustworthy pilot analyzes the situation to discover why the SOP didn't work and looks for ways to amend the SOP accordingly.

A "Big Picture" Focus

A humble pilot realizes that the higher goal of aviation is to accomplish all flight objectives without hurting anyone or breaking anything; as well as the personal goal of becoming a better pilot so as to achieve the higher goal more consistently.

An arrogant pilot doesn't understand why things cannot be perfect when they can point to so many of their personal accomplishments (while ignoring their many shortcomings).

The humble pilot understands that there is a cause and effect for all results; is truthful enough to understand that he or she is often the cause, and can be relied upon to keep this attitude at all times. In other words, this pilot has the big picture.

[www.dictionary.com]

[Items in blue are my comments.]

6: Ivan

Soviet Mig-25 Foxbat (USAF Photo)

I've always been a fan of beer call, a uniquely Air Force tradition where you end the day with a beer or three to hash out the day's victories against the defeats. You had a chance to regale your peers with the good – "The sky was inscribed with my name today!" – as well as the bad – "There I was, flat on my back, out of airspeed and ideas."

Beer call was fun at pilot training where all students had a natural bond against the insurmountable odds. Beer call was satisfying in all my previous flying squadrons where the workload was high but everyone was in it together. Beer call at the 89th was something foreign to me. It was an hour of politics, to see and to be seen. It was also expected after a check ride, good or bad.

"You owe me a beer," Hank Richards said.

"Because I passed?" I asked.

"No," he said. "Because you didn't fail. I was betting heavy on your bust, all the signs were there. Oh well. Where's my beer?"

That was the general consensus. Stan/Evil was denied their humbling bust but could not be denied forever. "You aren't really a SAM Fox aircraft commander until the line check," Hank said. "Those can be pretty easy for someone like you, it all depends on where they send you."

"Where did you go?" I asked.

"London and back," he said with a laugh. "Everyone thought I won the lottery. Two legs! And to England of all places! It doesn't get any easier."

The aircraft commander upgrade check proved I was in command of the machine. The line check would prove I was in command of the crew and the mission. England and back would be easy, I knew. But I also knew the SAM Mafia would ensure I would get something a bit tougher. It was a topic for another day. Having shown my face and having bought myself and someone else a beer, I headed for the parking lot. I felt a tap on my shoulder just as I made it to the door. I turned to see Colonel William Edmonds.

"We need to talk," he said.

"Yes, sir," I said. I followed him out to the parking lot where he seemed to have a destination in mind. He was dressed in a coat and tie, fitting for a retired colonel and former commander of the 89th.

"They are very impressed with you, Eddie," he said. "They think you can go all the way."

"That's odd," I said. "I get the impression the SAM Mafia wanted me busted today."

"The SAM Mafia did," he said. "But you beat them and that's yet another reason they are impressed."

"All this time I thought 'they' and the 'SAM Mafia' were one and the same," I said.

"Not even close," he said. "The SAM Mafia are just the people who run this wing and that changes every time the airlines start hiring. The SAM Mafia used to be the finest pilots in the world and that made them the safest. *Experto Crede* meant something back then."

"And now?"

"Now?" He stopped and glanced over his shoulder, back to the Officer's Club. "In any Air Force wing you have three tiers of pilots. You gotcher top aces, you gotcher average sticks, and you gotcher dregs. The trouble is the airlines hadn't hired for so long that our top aces got to be too good. They started beating up on everyone else. That went on for years. Now the airlines hired away our top aces and our average pilots. So that left the dregs that got turned down by the airlines as our top tier. They won't be around forever. The 89th is coming back. That's why they have so much invested in you. Understand?"

"Yes, sir."

Edmonds extended his hand and I shook it. He turned one-eighty and returned to the O'Club. I scanned the parking lot and found my truck.

Three days later I was strapped into another Gulfstream with four senators and five staffers in back, on our way to negotiate a peace treaty between Azerbaijan and Armenia. The two countries had splintered away from the USSR, the Union of Soviet Socialist Republics, and decided to duke it out with fifty-year old tanks and whatever leftover Russian weaponry they could get their hands on.

Up front I had Captain Michael Houghton in the right seat. He was the sharpest captain in our class of recently hired 89th pilots. He would fly the entire trip from the right seat as I earned my right to become a SAM Fox aircraft commander, provided Lieutenant Colonel Shannon agreed. Shannon strapped into the jump seat and tapped me on the shoulder.

"Is this airplane within authorized weight and balance limitations?" he asked.

"Balance, yes," I said, "weight, no. The passengers showed up with bulletproof vests, survival gear, and a lot of bottled water. We are probably exceeding the baggage compartment limits by a thousand pounds."

"Very well," he said. Houghton grinned as he busied himself with the before starting engines checklist. Now we three pilots were all complicit in our small bit of SAM Fox. Shannon and Houghton, I am sure, believed it was because this was a mission of national importance worthy of bending the aircraft limitations. As for me, I just wanted to pass the check ride.

The check ride had been hastily arranged. On Monday the warring countries agreed to the United States as an impartial arbiter and the Senate Foreign Affairs committee selected peace negotiators from its ranks. On Tuesday the squadron got the mission and the SAM Fox Mafia selected me for the mission and Shannon as the designated hit man. I spent that evening with the base intelligence office, learning just how serious the Russians and ex-Russians were about the war.

"Whatever you do," the colonel in charge of the intel shop said, "you stay out of Nagorno-Karbakh. The Azerbaijanis got it, the people who live there want out and the Armenians are all too happy to make that happen. We figured your flight plan from Germany through Russia and to Azerbaijan and Armenia. Your exit is off to a U.S. base in Turkey. You stick to those courses and you'll be okay."

I had a stack of Air Force Intelligence approved flight plans and IFR route charts in my briefcase. In our aircraft safe I had a stack of Central Intelligence Agency reports for every country along our route of flight with specific warnings not to overfly Azerbaijan and Armenia – there was a war going on, after all – and another report saying we could ignore those warnings because of our unique role as peacekeepers.

Our first leg was a fuel stop in Gander, Newfoundland. The flight was less than 3 hours, but the stop was needed because the next leg to Frankfurt, Germany would take another 6 hours. We showed up for duty 3 hours prior to departure, it took about 30 minutes to refuel in Gander, and another hour in Germany. By the time we left for our final leg of the day, we had been on duty for almost 14 hours and still had at least another 5 to go.

I looked to my right. Mike Houghton slumped in his seat, his right arm against the window, propping up a heavy head. He looked tired. "You okay?"

"Yeah," he said. "We had a 16 hour limit in the C-141. These 20 hour days take some getting use to."

"And you're just a kid," I said. "It only gets worse." I was tired too, but I grew up in the part of the Air Force that pushed its pilots to the limits. The normal crew duty limit for a civilian crew of two pilots is typically 14 hours. Most Air Force crews used 16 hours. My previous squadrons used 18. The 89th used 18 hours but allowed the aircraft commander to waive that to 20 hours with no outside approval needed. I would be waiving those hours today.

I looked at our inertial navigation system and pressed the ETA button. "In another 4 hours and 10 minutes you can relax," I said.

Mike shrugged and picked up the flight plan, double-checking the fuel burn. He and I both knew it would take at least another hour on top of that 4 hours and 10 minutes to get the airplane secured and an hour more to find our way to the hotel and a nice, warm bed. The thought was comforting.

"Sam shest nol dva! Sam shest nol dva! Zapretnyeff! Oborot totchas zhe!"

What was that?

"Sam shest nol dva! Sam shest nol dva! Zapretnyeff! Oborot totchas zhe!"

It sounded Russian. I knew what Sam was, that was our call sign, Special Air Missions, SAM 602. "Dva" is two, I remembered that from Prisoner of War school. I was prisoner number two, "zhivotnyeff dva." Sam shest nol dva. Nul is zero in a few languages; I suppose "nol" could be zero. It had to be. "Sam shest nol dva" was "Sam Six Zero Two."

Why was someone yelling at me in Russian?

"Sam shest nol dva! Sam shest nol dva! Zapretnyeff! Oborot totchas zhe!"

My head dropped back and hit the headrest on the seat, causing my headset to fall around my neck. I opened my eyes and in a few seconds was transported from my bed to the left seat of our Gulfstream III. We were at 40,000 feet somewhere over Russia. I looked around. The copilot was sound asleep and so was the engineer. What about the radio operator? I pressed the "RO" button on my interphone panel while shaking the copilot's left arm.

"Pilot, this is radio, what's up?"

"Listen to VHF one."

Mike Houghton put on his best "I was only resting my eyes" act while shuffling his fuel log and the en route chart. The engineer continued to snooze blissfully.

"Pilot he is saying Sam Six Zero Two," the radio operator said over the interphone. "Let me see if I got any of that other stuff in my phrase book." Master Sergeant Steve Queen was the best in the business but I didn't expect him to be fluent in Russian.

"Where are we, Mike?"

The copilot pushed the "Lat/Long" button on our inertial reference computer and thumbed through the en route chart. "Right here," he said, his finger on an airway we've never used before. Most of this airspace was hours inside the Iron Curtain, hours behind the "DO NOT ENTER, AIRCRAFT WILL BE FIRED UPON" warnings on the chart.

"Radio, pilot," Steve called.

"Go."

"I don't have any of those words in my book, pilot, but he sounds really pissed. Is that the guard frequency?"

"It is," I said. The Russians had just recently added our western guard frequency, 121.5, to their radar control sites. And now they were using it. The fact we had signed diplomatic clearances from the Russian government onboard gave me little comfort. Getting shot down wasn't part of the program but nobody on the airplane spoke Russian.

I traced our route of flight along the en route chart and examined the name of every radio beacon, every town, and every printed name. "Nizhnevartovsk," I said aloud, "that sounds familiar. Anybody recognize it?"

"Tom Clancy, pilot." Steve had left his radio operator cubicle and was now leaning over the flight engineer, still happily sleeping.

"What?"

"It was in Tom Clancy's latest novel; the one about the Russians marching to the English Channel in a few days. I don't remember what was special about the town, but the next war starts because of something in that town."

"Sam shest nol dva! Sam shest nol dva! Zapretnyeff! Oborot totchas zhe!"

"Well, so be it," I said. I uncoupled the autopilot from the navigation system and turned the airplane ninety degrees to the left. "Let's give this town a wide berth. We got enough fuel to go two hundred miles around it?"

Mike fumbled with his fuel log and I did some quick math. Two hundred miles north, two hundred miles south was about an hour. The fuel flow gauges were showing about 2,100 pounds per hour each, so this was going to cost us about 4,000 pounds of fuel. I always took off with the maximum, either the most we could get off the ground with or the maximum we could land with. It should be okay.

"We'll be okay," Mike said, "if we don't get shot down."

Indeed. Mike kept studying the chart while I pulled out the flight plan computed for us by the good folks at Jeppesen and approved by our base intel shop. Our original course line was just as planned and approved.

"Hear that?" Steve asked.

"What?"

"Ivan's quiet," he said.

The guard frequency was silent. After thirty minutes we turned right and another thirty minutes after that right again. After an hour and a half we turned left and were on course to Azerbaijan again.

"Pilot, radio, I got some intel guy on the satellite. Button seventeen on your panel."

"This is Major Haskel, go ahead."

"What the hell are you guys doing up there? The Kremlin is pissed, the White House is pissed, and that means I'm pissed. Don't you know you can't fly over the Anti-Ballistic Missile site at Nizhnevartovsk?"

"First of all," I said in my faux calm voice - the one I used whenever I'm getting yelled at, it makes the person doing the yelling even angrier - "I never heard of the place until a couple of hours ago. Secondly, it was on our flight plan. And my third point, the one you should be interested in, your office approved the flight plan."

There was a moment of silence; I thought we had lost the connection. Then he came back. "Oh, I see that. Well, don't over-fly it again." And with a click the frequency went dead. Two hours later Shannon reappeared from either a nap or a prolonged flirting session with the flight attendant. An hour after that we were on the ground in Azerbaijan, the airplane surrounded by a squad of Russian guards. After another hour to clear customs and more Russian guards, we were stuffed into a pint-sized van headed to Baku, the capital city.

It had once been a magnificent hotel, constructed back in the days when marble was cheap and labor was cheaper. It had huge columns inside and out, and the lobby ceilings were at least thirty feet high. The furniture was elegant and ornate. Well, it was once elegant. Now everything was faded and dingy, even the people.

Even after spending nineteen hours in the airplane in coat and tie wishing my neck was free of its tourniquet, I somehow ended in bed, fully clothed, tie included. I woke to the click, click, clicking of my own teeth, chattering their enamel away in an attempt to generate some body heat. Breakfast was inedible, all ten courses of it. I managed to stomach half a cup of the syrupy coffee and made plans to get to the airplane early enough to brew an American pot of good ol' Folgers. I was first in the lobby, an hour early, eager to leave this tomb of a hotel. I set an 8 a.m. show time for the rest of the crew and normally showed up thirty early. Most SAM crews knew that fifteen early was the minimum. As the aircraft commander, I had to be first. But I was never an hour early.

I was soon in good company. Mike trudged down the long staircase at forty early. His coat and tie looked worse than mine. If it weren't for the new shirt, I would say he hadn't changed at all.

"You sleep in that?"

"Yeah," he said, "good morning to you too."

One-by-one, everyone made it to the lobby early. Shannon looked marginally better than Mike and I. Ed, the flight engineer, came into the lobby with a bang, his rollaway suitcase breaking free of his grasp and leaping the last ten or twenty steps solo. He started to curse the %$#@! Russian staircase and the %$#@! Russian marble, and the...

"Sergeant Ugly American?" I asked. He restrained the rest of his tirade.

Steve, the radio operator, showed up as if he had the best sleep of his life and looked no different than after his layover on our last trip together, at LAX I think. His compartment on our Gulfstream was the only enclosed space on the airplane, built from a closet and lined with his electronic gizmos. I know the passengers slept most of the way over and he didn't have much to do. He had probably slept too.

Tina was last, as required by the flight attendant job description, and looked like a million rubles, as usual. No evidence of hypothermia with her. Having lugged her bags all over the world I suspected she had her own campfire stove and goose down comforter in one of her two suitcases.

We sat in silence until our embassy driver showed, and then again in silence on the drive to the airport. It was our first look at the city in daylight, or some Russian facsimile for daylight. A blanket of smog turned whatever sunrays were able to penetrate into a diffuse glow with no source whatsoever. Every building was built in the same once-magnificent style, devoid of any paint for decades.

"Look at the grass," Steve said pointing through a dirty window, "I've never seen grass that color."

"What color is that?"

"Gray," we all said at once.

The drive to the airport was along the Caspian Sea. It too was gray. On our approach in the darkness yesterday over that very body of water we lost all navigation signals and had to set the height of the nearest obstacles as our minimum descent altitude. Now, in the semi-lightness of the day we could see those obstacles for the first time: a sea of gray oil derricks. Steve and Ed traded stories about the oil derricks in Texas and Tina joined in with her Lone Star stories. Mike and I locked eyes on the derricks, thinking back to yesterday's uncertain approach into the darkness.

The enlisted crewmembers chatted happily for a while until they too fell silent. We entered the airport compound and got our first real glimpse of the control tower and airport terminal; half a terminal, really. The entire western side of the building was missing and you could see the insides of offices, hallways, stairwells, and even bathrooms. "What the . . ." Ed began to say until he caught my glance.

"It was the Armenians," our embassy driver said, "the war has been very bad. But now is better. The enemy is several kilometers west by now. No danger."

"No danger," I repeated for the rest of the crew. "We are invited guests of both governments. No worries."

I pulled Steve to one side. "As soon as you get to the airplane, fire up all that comm gear and call Whamo. Tell them that if we don't have a diplomatic clearance into Armenia we aren't going." Whamo, the White House Military Office, was our connection into the world of foreign diplomacy and border clearances.

"Yes, sir," he said. "Is that a bluff?" Bluffing, all our radio operators knew, was the number one tool in our bag of tricks. We were allowed to throw the White House's clout around, make threats, offer bribes; we could do whatever it took to keep the mission on schedule. It was almost always enough to get the job done.

"No," I answered. "Those Armenians shot down a Russian airliner last year. I'm not messing with them."

Our pretty blue, gold, and white Gulfstream was where we had left it, still surrounded by KGB. There appeared to be fifteen of them. All our squadron's aircraft had diplomatic status. The "United States of America" painted on either side meant wherever it flew, a part of the U.S. was en route. The KGB couldn't board the airplane. But they could keep us out of it if they wanted.

"Passport control," the guard in front said, "no entry. Passport control."

"KGB," Steve said.

"$#@! KG used to be," Ed began and ended as his eyes caught my glare.

We drove to the bombed-out side of the terminal and found ourselves walking up a zig-zag stairwell, every other zig was in the open air where the wall once was. We ended on an upper floor and down a dark, poorly lit corridor. A naked bulb strung on a makeshift wire nailed to the side of the surviving wall lit our way, every twenty or thirty feet. We marched down the hallway, single file; the click, click of our heels muffled by dirt, trash, and rat droppings. At last we came to a corner and turned to see two more Russian guards standing at attention. These were cheaper versions of those around the airplane. Their uniforms were a drab brown with no ornamentation other than red epaulets on each shoulder, each with a single diagonal stripe.

Each guard remained erect at attention as we approached, each eyeing me suspiciously, but not moving otherwise. I rapped my knuckles against the door twice, as instructed by our embassy driver. A sliding window, just wide enough for a pair of eyes, opened. Two eyes appeared and the slit closed again. A chain was unchained, a lock was unlocked, and the door opened. We walked into a barren room populated only by a desk, an enormous woman in uniform on the other side, and one empty chair opposite her. Hers was the same uniform as those surrounding our airplane, with diamonds on the red epaulettes and a silver badge of some sort on her ample chest. She was flanked by two more army types, dressed like the ones outside, but these with two diagonal stripes on each epaulette.

"Please to sit, kapitan."

I sat as instructed and handed over our six green, diplomatic passports. She eyed each carefully. She read each once, starting with mine on top, then the others, and then returned to mine. I was born in Tokyo, Japan and in some parts of the world that garnered a second look. We were all very silent. I could hear Ed's labored breathing and said a silent prayer that he would keep his mouth shut. The guards too were silent. As I waited, I noticed their trigger fingers were actually on the triggers of their rifles. In the U.S. military we were taught to keep our fingers off the trigger unless getting ready to shoot.

The female army type looked up from our passports and directly into my eyes. "You are American Army, yes?"

"No," I said with a serious face, "American Air Force. We are not ugly enough to be American Army."

I could hear Tina's gasp. For a few seconds there was no sound whatsoever. I suddenly thought about those trigger fingers and about a counseling session I got years ago as a cadet about the drawbacks of a dry sense of humor.

During those interminable seconds her faced portrayed no emotion. The neurons dedicated to the English-to-Russian translation were busy at work and finally the task was done. Her faced erupted with a smile and her laughter bellowed through the room. She said something to the two guards flanking her and they too broke out with laughter.

"You may pass, American Air Force, you may pass."

Our passengers arrived early, apparently eager to leave one hellhole for another. We popped out of the smog about 1,000 feet above the terrain and headed southwest to Armenia. Yerevan sits just north of Mount Ararat, where the Bible tells us Noah's Ark ended after 40 days of rain. With an elevation of 16,854 feet above sea level, it poses the largest threat to an approach into Zvartnots Airport, at a mere 2,841 feet.

The terminal weather frequency was half Russian, half broken English; but the news was clear enough.

"Visibility is at 400 meters," Mike said. "Good enough, but just barely. We studied the most complicated approach chart either of us had ever seen and tuned what needed to be tuned. Mike taped a meters-to-feet conversion table to his right and an altimeter QFE to QNH chart to his yoke. The Russians would be expecting us to fly in meters and would be issuing altimeter settings based on field elevation (QFE) and not mean sea level (QNH). We had more than a few opportunities to mess this up.

As I pulled the throttles aft for our descent, Shannon replaced Ed in the engineer's seat and the smell of Tina's perfume wafted forward. Shannon was married, I knew. "Figures," I said to myself quietly.

"What?" he asked.

"Nothing," I said.

We knew air traffic control from one country would not be talking with the next so I contacted Armenia on a separate radio as Mike worked with Azerbaijan on our normal ATC radio. As we left his airspace, the Azerbaijani controller simply said, "Good bye, Sam." Mike switched frequencies.

"Whoa!" Shannon said from the jump seat. "Are you going to cross this border without clearance from the next country? I can't let you do that!"

I gave Mike a wink and he dialed in the frequency I had been using. "Good morning, Sam," the new controller said. "Welcome to Armenia. Cleared to

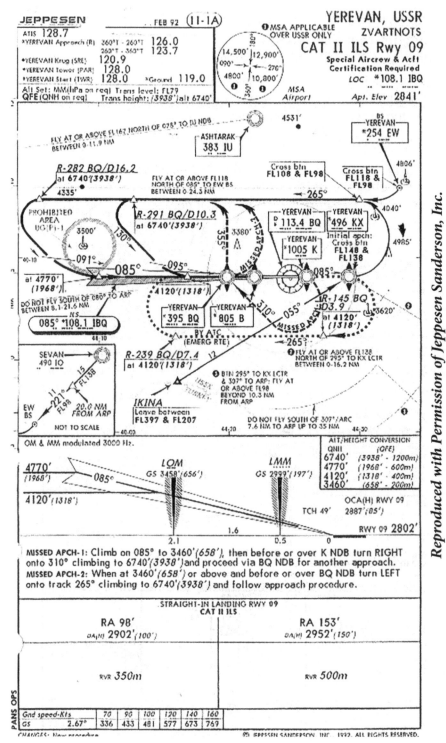

the Echo Whiskey beacon. We have no radar, you are cleared to navigate according to the ILS, runway zero nine, category two approach. Call me established inbound." Mike smiled and Shannon fell suddenly quiet.

The approach either requires a lot of math or "dive and drive" descents while navigating fix-to-fix in a box pattern. I did the math, programmed a few cheats into the inertial navigation system, and let Mike know exactly what I had planned. Shannon, our examiner, had been in back with the flight attendant and was in the dark. He managed to keep silent until our last instruction from approach control after Mike made our inbound call.

"Sam you are cleared to descend to 400 meters," the controller said, "and you are cleared for the ILS category two, runway zero nine approach." Mike acknowledged the clearance and dialed 4,200 feet into our autopilot's altitude select window.

"Four hundred," Shannon said. Mike pulled the approach plate from his yoke and pointed to the meters-to-feet and then the QFE-to-QNH conversion. "Oh."

We made the evaluator look bad twice in one flight, I thought. That can't be good. For a moment, however, I did have my doubts. Once the ILS glide slope needle started its march from the top of its scale, I felt better. An ILS is an ILS, even in Russia.

Zvartnots had the look of an old Russian bomber base: long runways constructed of concrete blocks with wide gaps every ten meters or so. The wheels kissed the concrete only to be slapped at every gap. The gaps slowed the airplane without needing any braking and we found ourselves in a second former Russian republic with a new set of guards without the Russian uniforms. The passengers were escorted away to Yerevan, the capital city of Armenia. We found ourselves in another unheated hotel with more inedible food. While Baku was notable because of the absence of color, Yerevan's defining characteristic was tree stumps. "Only way to heat," our driver told us, "all the trees are gone. We must burn furniture next."

"Everyone get some sleep," I told the crew as we stood with the huge skeleton keys to our rooms. They all looked as beat as I felt. "I need to spend some time on the airplane's phone tomorrow, so let's bypass the hotel's breakfast and see if we can talk Tina into some real food."

"I was going to suggest that," Tina said. "How does steak and eggs sound?"

"Perfect," I said. "Steve, we still don't have diplomatic clearance to cross into

Turkey tomorrow. You need to fire up all the electrons you got, as soon as we get the airplane running."

"You got it, sir."

The next morning Tina was as good as her word and whipped up a six-course breakfast to make up for the missing meals since our arrival. Steve got a satellite connection with our trip coordinator at the Pentagon. Mr. Phelps, an aptly named impossible mission sort, didn't seem to care about our impending dead-in-the-water status.

I was at the midpoint of the cabin, in a seat of Steve's choosing. He connected the Pentagon phone to the phone in seat 4R. Tina presented my breakfast there and Ed ended up facing me at 3R. Steve took the seat opposite me and Shannon was opposite Ed. The only missing crewmember was Mike, who took his meal in the copilot's seat. I cradled the phone against my shoulder as I built an egg sandwich from the ingredients on the plate. Finally my phone connection came alive.

"We are supposed to carry a peacekeeping team from Armenia to Turkey tomorrow," I said, "but we don't have diplomatic clearances from either government."

"You can't fly from Armenia to Turkey," he said over the push-to-talk satellite connection. The single duplex phone meant only one of us could talk at a time while the other listened. "They are both looking for an excuse to start a shooting war. Over." Over the years the term "over" had been dropped, but novices with these systems couldn't resist.

"That's why I am calling you," I said. I flew my right hand over my head, gesturing to the crew. "You going to handle this, Mister Phelps?"

That chore done, I returned to my eggs. Just then there was a loud explosion and the ground beneath the airplane shuddered. Mike yelled from the cockpit. "You guys gotta see this."

The crew made its way to the cockpit and I plopped myself into the pilot's seat, egg sandwich in hand. Ahead of us in the distance, maybe a mile or two, there was a plume of black smoke billowing against the dirty blue sky. "What caused that?"

"A Sukhoi," Mike answered, "or maybe it was a Mig."

"You shitting me?" Ed was crouched between us, craning his neck skyward. "A Russian fighter?"

Before Mike could answer we saw the evidence screaming against the horizon to our left. The fighter swooped down towards the original plume and released another bomb. We saw a second plume and a few seconds later heard the loud kaboom as the airplane pulled up and zoomed out of our sight.

"What are you going to do if he shows up again tomorrow?" Shannon asked. The question obviously directed to me. It was a ridiculous question. What could we do?

"Okay," I said with the somber air required by the situation, "here's the plan." The crew listened intently; I had the stage to myself. "If the fighters are still here tomorrow we'll takeoff as scheduled. If that fighter comes up, I'll execute a scissors maneuver and get Ivan right into our six o'clock position." I demonstrated with my hands crisscrossing each other and finally with one behind the other. Mike suppressed a grin. "Tina, I'll call back to the galley. At the last minute, I'll press hard left rudder and put Ivan off to our left. Tina will open the microwave door and put the oven on Hi and press start. Thirty years from now Ivan will get cancer. Boy will he be sorry."

Everyone just stood there in silence. Their faces scanned the gamut from abject horror to stunned dismay.

"Don't worry about it, guys." Wow, I didn't expect that. "Steve, get me our White House military contact on the phone."

Ivan was news to the White House too. We stayed in the airplane with the APU running for another five hours, waiting for the return phone call. Tina and Ed played cards, Steve read, Shannon napped, while Mike and I sat in the cockpit and talked.

"Are we really going to take off with fighters in the air?" Mike still had the hint of a grin on his face.

"Of course not."

Just after lunch was served, our phone call came in. "We got your clearance to leave tomorrow, major." The caller was from the White House military office, an annex building adjoining the big white building on Pennsylvania Avenue. He kept his side of the phone keyed so I couldn't interject the obvious question. "Your Armenian clearance number is four, seven, oscar, alpha, two, one. Your Turkish clearance number is tomorrow's date followed by sierra, alpha, mike. So now you have what you need, right?" He released his end of the conversation.

"What about the fighter strafing the airport?" I released my push-to-talk button, thinking the word 'strafe' might not be accurate.

"Oh yeah," he answered, "turns out that was strictly for your benefit. It was a single fighter sent to the airport just to let your passengers know the bad guys could reach them if they wanted to."

"Who are the bad guys?"

"Who, indeed. Don't worry about it major, both sides agree the sky belongs to you tomorrow."

After another night in our hotel with no heat and restaurant with no food, we collected our passengers and left. There was no Russian fighter and no need to execute my brilliantly conceived scissors maneuver.

Three days later we were back at Andrews, each of us with a commendation letter for a job well done avoiding the ABM site and getting the peacekeepers to where they needed to be and back without a scratch. Lieutenant Colonel Tim Shannon, commendation letter in hand, had no choice but to pass me and herald me into the ranks of SAM Fox aircraft commanders.

Returning from a two-week trip I expected a stack of mail in the squadron and at home and wasn't disappointed. The only surprise was a business card with the photo of a United Airlines Boeing 737 and the name "Captain Kevin Davies" with an Alexandria, Virginia address. Kevin and I were pilot training buddies in Arizona and squadron mates in Hawaii. He had jumped to the airlines just six years ago.

"Captain Davies?" I asked after he picked up the phone on the second ring. "Is United getting desperate?"

"Yeah," he said, "they hand out the four stripes to anyone these days."

Kevin was hired just after the major airlines really understood how deregulation was going to impact the industry and just before a huge hiring influx. He got in before the rush and that meant he would never see a furlough if his airline managed to survive. "It was easy," he explained. "I sat sideways for nine months, engineer on Boeing 747s. Then five years as a copiglet on the 737 and now the Supreme Being on the same jet. I bet my pay is double yours."

"Triple," I said. "But you don't get all the fun and adventure, so we're even." I gave him the Reader's Digest version of my upgrade check rides, the ABM over-flight, and the Russian fighter.

"Those Russians don't mess around," he said.

"Korean Airlines double oh seven," I said.

"More than that," he said. "They've shot down three airliners in the last twenty years. You engineers really ought to study more history."

Intercept Avoidance / Missile Evasion

Key: Overflight Permit required ■ No permit required Current Airspace Warnings

World Overflight Map (Flight Service Bureau, as of 6 August 2016)

Intercept Avoidance

Intelligence. The best way to avoid being intercepted, fired upon, and shot down is to avoid areas where they do that sort of thing in the first place. Unfortunately, the list of "bad actors" is increasing and ever changing. It really pays to have someone on your payroll who keeps track of this in real time. I use the Flight Service Bureau (www.fsbureau.org). They send emails, almost on a daily basis, letting you know where the trouble spots are. (The "trouble" can be more than just a country throwing missiles into air routes, it can include volcano eruptions, ATC strikes, or anything else that would ruin your flight in international airspace.)

Fly Common Well-Traveled Routing. There are some countries in the world where flying off airways can get you in big trouble. Just because a country's ATC clears you direct to your destination doesn't mean the country's air force will be informed that you mean no offense to anyone. Consult your aeronautical information publications to be sure. But when in doubt, stick to the roads most frequently traveled.

Stay on Course. Once en route, keep the navigation needles centered. There is a school of thought that preaches using a Strategic Lateral Offset Procedure (SLOP) in domestic airspace in countries where some of the air traffic may not always be at the correct altitude. Very few countries permit SLOP in non-oceanic or remote airspace.

Light Up, Squawk, Transmit. Let everyone know you are a civilian, unarmed, passenger or cargo carrying aircraft – not a spy plane. Fly with as many lights as your aircraft permits without performance limitations. Squawk the appropriate ATC code. Clearly annunciate your call sign to make it clear you are a civilian aircraft. If you have a company assigned call sign that sounds hostile (Killer 21, for example), change it to your registration number. (Make sure your Mode-S and data link agree.)

Monitor Guard. Very few countries require you to monitor a guard frequency except when flying oceanic. An interceptor, however, is taught to try that frequency first. It is a good idea to monitor guard frequency anywhere in the world where there is even the slightest chance you might be intercepted.

121.5 MHz – this frequency is 'guarded' by many ATC stations and many military aircraft; in some countries it can be given other names, such as the "Distress and Diversion" frequency.

243.0 MHz – this frequency is 'guarded' by many ATC stations and many military aircraft.

Missile Evasion

It has been said that firing an AIM 9 Sidewinder missile at an airplane is the same thing as saying, "I wish you were dead," because it was almost a certain kill. But nothing is 100% certain and if you find yourself with a missile headed your way, you do have a few options. A fighter pilot friend of mine elaborates . . .

[Chris Didier]

Interesting Q regarding a missile defense on a transport jet. To be blunt, there's very little a pilot can do flying a limited maneuvering jet against a Mach 3+ missile that can make 22G+ turns. With that said, there are two schools of thought: try to out run/out maneuver or take the hit from a stable platform. First some academics . . .

Missiles from the surface or aerial adversary are generally one of two types: radar or optical guided. Optical can be of various sorts, but most are tracking a heat source (engine exhaust if behind, skin friction if in front). Heat seeking missiles are typically smaller, accelerate faster, and are harder to see. Radar guided missiles are typically larger, leaving a larger smoke trail and many have a booster section that jettisons just before a 2nd stage motor fires. Time of Flight (TOF) for heat seeking missiles are usually shorter than radar guided. Unless a pilot can recognize the missile trajectory, boosted phases, smoke trail, etc, it is common practice to be in idle to minimize heat signature (assume the missile is heat seeking). Otherwise, keep the power at max to minimize airspeed loss if maneuvering to avoid a stall.

Back to the two schools of thought. Maneuvering can possibly generate an acceptable miss distance to reduce the missile's effective probability of kill (Pk). Downsides are overspeeding or overstressing your aircraft (over-G). If the missile does impact causing damage, having excessive speeds or G-loading may exacerbate aircraft damage from the missile. A slower and stable (wings level) platform would likely absorb the effects of damage better from the missile impact. Ultimately, it comes down to the pilot's assessment of the situation. Basically, if a missile is fired with a short TOF (<10 sec) and it appears out maneuvering is very unlikely, it would be best to stay stable, in idle power and ~5 degrees nose down. Otherwise . . .

A pilot attempting to out-maneuver a missile must respect the aircraft's limits, mostly airspeed and G-loading (i.e. take it to the edge but not past). When an air-to-air missile is fired from a great distance, the easiest way to recognize them are contrails that appear to be arcing in the horizon. All missile shots at range typically loft and will make contrails. Surface-to-air missiles tend to be shot inside their max range to reduce TOF and detection. The first thought a crew member may have is, "Holy cow, is this country launching a rocket into space?" To me, the SA-2/SA-3 looked just like a Space Shuttle launch (seen both in person). The good news is there is time; their TOFs can range from 30-90 seconds. There are several types of guidance modes for radar missiles. Most common are command guided, proportional or semi-proportional and appear to track differently on your windscreen. To keep it simple, let's describe a trajectory like skeet or trap shooting. Most guided missiles will initially aim for where you are flying and "meet halfway." In all cases, how a pilot maneuvers can greatly reduce the missile's energy.

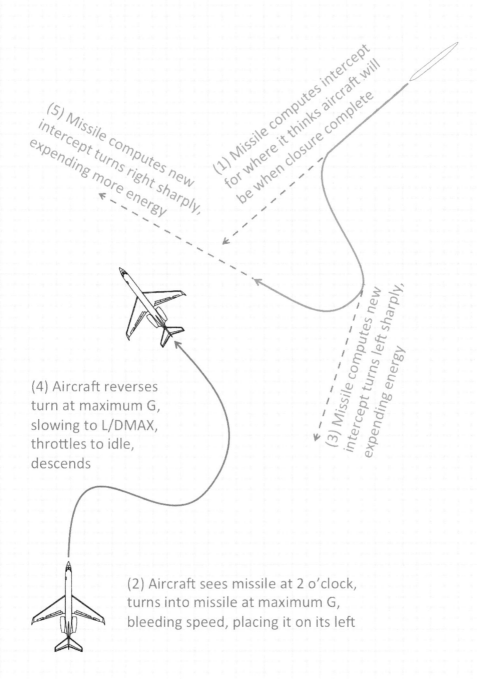

(5) Missile computes new intercept turns right sharply, expending more energy

(1) Missile computes intercept for where it thinks aircraft will be when closure complete

(3) Missile computes new intercept turns left sharply, expending energy

(4) Aircraft reverses turn at maximum G, slowing to L/DMAX, throttles to idle, descends

(2) Aircraft sees missile at 2 o'clock, turns into missile at maximum G, bleeding speed, placing it on its left

103

Let's describe a scenario. If you see a missile fired at you from RIGHT 2 o'clock, position, it will be aiming for an intercept ahead of you off your nose. To deplete the missile's energy, make a hard RIGHT turn past it and put it at your LEFT 9 to 10 o'clock, roll out then descend ~15 deg with idle power. It will force the missile to turn harder (b/c it's going so damn fast), correct its intercept point and deplete energy (watch out for your overspeed). After you see the missile correct its course, reverse hard LEFT turn to put the missile back at your RIGHT 2 to 3 o'clock position and roll out with full power and ~5 deg climb (watch out for over-G). Again the missile must make a correction. These maneuvers can be accomplished at level flight but adding the 3rd dimension of alternating descents and climbs (at any +/- pitch) will add to the missile intercept problem. Maneuvering properly and assuming a long missile TOF, you may see the missile stall before impact (best case) or the missile avoiding impact during its final turn correction (less than best case). Keep in mind, most missiles have proximity fusing. They are smart enough to detonate at the closest point of intercept if the missile determines impact is impossible. So if you feel impact (or near miss) is imminent, strive to return to wings level and ~5-deg nose low.

Turning into the missile will be a hard thing to do if you've never done this for a living (like Chris) and you are likely to be frozen with shock for a while. But you need to do it. Using the maximum G your airplane has available will do two things for you: it will force the missile to make the largest correction and it will bleed off your cruise speed. Once the missile is on your opposite side, reverse the turn. Because you will have lost some speed your turn radius will be tighter, but the missile will be closer, so once again apply maximum G. For this turn, keep an eye on your angle of attack. Most aircraft will have a maximum lift-to-drag ratio at 0.30 angle of attack and this is a good number to shoot for. You can also look at airspeed (if you have an instantaneous VREF readout, use that), but keep in mind your stall speed goes up with G-force. Your objective is to end this maneuver as slow as the airplane can fly with adequate controllability. So if all this maneuvering failed to shake the missile, you will be in the best condition to survive a missile impact and/or detonation.

[Chris Didier, Lieutenant Colonel, USAF – Retired F-15E Instructor Pilot, interview 6 August 2016]

[Items in blue are my comments.]

7: Patriot Blue

Marine One en route to the White House (Department of Defense photo)

The best job in the squadron had to be as a fully qualified aircraft commander turned loose on trips with other fully qualified aircraft commanders. You didn't have to put up with an instructor pilot, the ever-present grade book, and the relentless critiques.

"You and me," I said to my favorite scheduler. "Come on Hank, you can make that happen."

Hank turned his 3-ring scheduling book around and pointed to a beautiful trip to Cyprus. Next to his name was an erasure under which the outlines of the name "Haskel" could be seen. "I already thought of that, Eddie. But it wasn't to be." He pulled out another book marked "TOP SECRET, NO FORN, PATRIOT BLUE" and turned to a new scheduling page I had never seen before. "Show up at building 213 tomorrow at 0700. Pack for four days, warm weather. Wear your dress blues, short sleeves, and tie. Don't mention this to anyone unless you know they have the same code word."

In a second the mysterious book was gone and Hank resumed his usual banter with the rest of the crew dogs politicking for trips, pretending the secret scheduling book didn't exist. I was left in the middle of the room with no one to talk to and no idea what to do next. Patriot Blue was the code word for White House missions, a part of my former life flying the Boeing 747. Once I left that life I was told to never breathe a word of it again. The penalty was death. "Or worse," we used to joke.

Most civilians realize there are secrets and there are top secrets. They don't realize that there are levels of secrets below that, such as "Confidential." Even in the military a vast majority of officers are granted only a "Secret" security clearance. Those with a special need can be granted "Top Secret" and those with access to nuclear weapons were part of a "Personnel Reliability Program," or PRP. What most people in the military didn't realize is that there are levels of secrets even higher, levels so high that even what they were called was considered too classified to utter in public. These "code word" clearances gave the owner access to a specific compartment of information. In a previous life I had access to the "Patriot Blue" compartment. But all of that was history, or so I thought.

The next morning I showed up at the appointed hour to the appointed place. It was a standard Air Force brown building with no identifying signs, other than the sterile "213" building number stenciled on one corner. The building was very close to a taxiway, but the taxiway did not appear on our airfield diagrams. The parking lot opposite the taxiway had seven vehicles, three of which had officer level decals. A barbed wire fence with the standard "Use of Deadly Force Authorized" signs went from one side of the building and along a twenty-foot buffer zone around to the other side of the building. The gate in front opened into an entrapment area. I walked into the open first gate, which immediately closed behind me.

The double entrapment, I knew, was to keep anyone approaching the building under control. I recognized the bulletproof glass around the guard shack and tried to keep my eyes from focusing on the gun ports and the rifle pointed my way. "Major Haskel," I said as I pushed my identity cards through the porthole. The guard picked up a phone and I waited. The rifle pointed in my direction relaxed.

A short but lean lieutenant colonel appeared from the building's front door and strode purposely towards us. He was wearing a gray flight suit I didn't recognize and other than his rank, there were no identifying patches. "Eddie," he said, "good to finally meet you. Come on in."

"We've never brought on a new pilot who already had his Patriot Blue," Lieutenant Colonel Paul Gables said as we entered the building. "So we are dispensing with all the training and putting you on duty with an instructor. You already know the Katz. He is looking forward to flying with you."

Lieutenant Colonel John P. Katzenberg was an early ally, but had never mentioned this secret alternative universe. We crossed what looked more like a living room from an old Ozzie and Harriet sitcom than an Air Force office and through a set of double doors into an airplane hangar. In there I saw two Gulfstreams, foreign to the Andrews fleet. One was painted just like our other Gulfstreams and the other was pure white, with no markings at all.

"So here comes your indoctrination," Gables said. "What does Patriot Blue mean to you?"

"Air Force One back up," I said.

"Right you are," he said. "Welcome home." He handed me three binders, each marked "Top Secret, No Forn" and each with their own code words. The Patriot Blue binder was on top. "The blue and white bird is yours, climb on board and start reading. But don't waste any time, wheels up in two hours."

Patriot Blue, in my former life, was our back up Boeing 747 shadowing the President to provide a ride if his airplane broke or he needed our special capabilities to fly anywhere in the world, nonstop. It would appear the program had much more to it than I previously knew. These hidden Gulfstreams provided an extra level of back up.

Other than a few extra toys, the cockpit looked like our non-secretive Gulfstreams. The cabin looked about the same as well, except for one unmistakable addition. Draped around the primary passenger's seat was the president's jacket. I eyed the presidential seal and reached to touch the name below, "President George . . ."

"We never say his name," I heard from behind me. It was John Katzenberg, the Katz. "To you and me he is 'Timberwolf.' That's what you are going to hear on the radio so you might as well get used to it. You know where we are going today, Eddie?"

"No," I said. "Good to see you, Katz."

"Likewise," he said. "Timberwolf is going to San Francisco today, and we are to remain within an hour of him at all times. We'll end up at NAS Alameda."

Katz explained that we would depart an hour early since we were so much slower than the President's Boeing 747. The big bird would pass us en route and we would land no earlier than 15 minutes after. Our airplane would be hidden at a Naval Air Station, out of sight and out of mind.

"Why haven't I ever heard about this operation before?" I asked.

"Only a third of the squadron knows we exist," he said. "I don't think anyone outside the squadron does. I'll fly west, you can fly us home."

An hour later we were airborne. The airplane was considerably heavier than what I was used to and the climb rate proved that fact. As we leveled off the expanded interphone panel came to life. First came the Secret Service chatter, then the President's helicopter, and finally Air Force One. Our secret radio frequencies were mostly quiet and the air traffic control frequencies seemed mundane as well. "They just declared their block time, Eddie."

I looked down to the radio operator's note and saw "AF-1 KSFO 2300Z" with a second line for us, "SAM-49 KNGZ 2315Z."

"We gotta make that happen," Katz said. "There is nothing worse than blowing your block time with the big boys watching."

"Eye wash," I thought but did not say. Even without any passengers our block time would be monitored and missing it would be a black mark on both our records. Cruising along at 36,000 feet our ground speed was only 350 knots; about 50 knots lower than planned. I compared the ETA column of our printed flight plan against the inertial navigation system; we were falling behind.

"I'm pushing point oh three," Katz said.

"Good idea," I said. It was our standard adjustment when late. We normally flew at 0.80 Mach, or eight-tenths the speed of sound. Flying at 0.83 Mach would cost us 300-pounds of fuel every hour, but save us 3-minutes every hour. I watched the speed increase, the ETA decrease, and the fuel flow dials rotate higher. Once everything settled, I recalculated.

"Still late," I said.

"Radio operator," he said over the interphone.

"Go, pilot," we heard in response.

"Call the Andrews weather shop, get me the winds at 36,000 feet from here to there."

"Get the winds for 32,000 feet too," I said. "In fact, throw in 28,000 feet."

"We'll burn too much gas at those altitudes," Katz said.

"Worth a look," I said.

In fifteen minutes we had our winds and it appeared we had another 1,000 nautical miles of the bad stuff. Our planned ground speed was 400 knots, but the winds would kick us down to only 350 knots. I spun the numbers on my circular slide rule. "We're losing 22 minutes," I said. Katz pushed the throttles forward. The Mach meter crept up to 0.845 and the groundspeed to 360 knots. The fuel flow meters jumped significantly. I spun the numbers again. "Good news, we are on time. Bad news, we will be a glider before we get there."

"Maybe Air Force One will adjust," Katz said. "They gotta be facing the same wind."

"Why don't we call them and ask?" I said. Our cockpit had a radio panel twice the size of the non-Presidential birds and one of those many radios was dedicated to Air Force One.

"Rule number one when you are the back up," he said, "is speak only when spoken to."

I looked at the radio operator's handwritten notes. The winds at 28,000 were 50 knots less. "Let's descend to 28,000, Katz. The winds are nicer down there."

"Fifty knots isn't enough," he said. "Besides, we burn more fuel down there."

"We get a higher true airspeed at 28,000," I said, "that might get us enough to pull the throttles back."

"Get us clearance," he said. "Worth a try."

Two radio calls later we were at 28,000 feet, flying Mach 0.80, and exceeding our planned 400 knots ground speed. "As soon as we are back on the time line," Katz said, "we'll pull it back to point seven, seven. Make back the gas."

By the time we got to the Rockies we were on time and on our gas curve. Katz lowered the airplane onto the Alameda runway precisely on time. "We got to add this trick to our squadron manual," he said. "Eddie, even the old heads are going to be impressed!"

Two days later Timberwolf was returning to D.C. and our extreme headwind became an extreme tailwind. Air Force One, for reasons only known to them, decided to keep their original block time. From the left seat I contemplated my options. "When in doubt," I said to myself, "do nothing."

We took off 15 minutes before the big Boeing and planned on landing 15 minutes after, but it wasn't working out. I kept the speed at Mach 0.80. "We could save some gas," Katz said from the right seat. "Your call."

"Let's wait a bit," I said. "I can't imagine what Air Force Once is doing flying so slowly. Something's not right."

I knew the Boeing 747 was most economical at Mach 0.86, just as our Gulfstream's best speed was Mach 0.80. But the big airplane also had a much larger speed margin. They could pull it back to Mach 0.70 or push it up to Mach 0.92. Our range was paltry by comparison. We could match the slow speed but anything faster than Mach 0.85 was out of the question.

"Pilot," the radio operator said over the interphone. "Colonel Benson on button seven."

I looked down at the interphone panel. That was Air Force One's frequency. Katz looked at me from the right seat. I was the pilot flying the airplane, but he was the pilot in command. "Well," he said, looking at me. "Don't keep the man waiting."

I selected button seven and keyed my microphone. "Yes sir, this is Major Haskel."

"Yeah," he said. "We need you to fly as fast as you can and give us a weather report after you land. Pass along a block time when you get it."

"Yes, sir," I said.

I pushed the interphone panel to release button seven and selected the radio operator's channel. "Please get me the Andrews weather."

"Already did," he said. "They are at minimums."

It didn't make any sense. "Air Force One has a category three ILS and we are only category two," I said cross-cockpit to Katz. "They have lower minimums than we do. What's the big deal?"

"Eddie, don't you know this yet?" Katz said. "If Andrews says the weather is at minimums, that means it is below minimums. It's a code to allow us to land no matter how bad the weather is. You should know that."

I guess I had heard that, but didn't believe it. In a sane world, the tower measures the ceiling and visibility so you know ahead of time if the weather is good enough to spot the runway and land. If the visibility wasn't good enough, there was no sense even attempting an approach. Most of the world uses a category one instrument landing system. The "Cat One" is good for 2,400-feet visibility, or as low as 1,800-feet given the right set of approach lights. In either case, the decision to land must be made no later than 200-feet above the runway. Since we were specially trained, our "Cat Two" minimums in the Air

Force got us down to 1,200-feet visibility and dropped our decision height to only 100-feet. Air Force One was good for "Cat Three" and had even lower visibility requirements. They didn't have a decision height to worry about.

"Why doesn't tower just tell them what the real weather is?" I asked. "They got the President on board, after all." My question wasn't worthy of an answer. I studied the Andrews ILS Category Two approach for Runway 01 Left with renewed interest. It was an easy approach, as these things go. Our autopilot was good enough to fly the approach, but not reliable enough to fly to minimums every single time. The SAM Fox rulebook said the approach had to be hand-flown.

"Speaking of things you should know," Katz said, "do you know about the 'smooth missed approach?'"

"Only ugly rumors," I said.

"We are not going to tell you to bust minimums," he said. "You know that. But a true SAM Fox pilot does everything smoothly, even the missed approach. If you don't see the runway at minimums but have all the needles centered, you can take it a little lower."

The entire foundation of instrument flying depended on a pilot immediately going around when at minimums without the runway in sight, there was no "smooth" about it. You shoved the power forward and pulled back on the yoke in an attempt to minimize altitude loss when close to the ground. With our Category II approach, we would be just 100 feet above the ground when starting the missed approach.

"How much lower?" I asked.

"That's your call," he said. "You are going to have the needles centered so you will be right over the runway. It really isn't a big deal."

"How can you guarantee you are going to be right over the runway?" I asked.

"If you are even one needle width off course, we'll go around," he said. "That guarantees it. You want me to fly it?"

"Of course not," I said, knowing that having him land the airplane from the right seat would be a sure admission that I wasn't up to SAM Fox standards.

"Just start the missed approach smoothly and allow the airplane to go a little lower. If you spot the runway, land."

That decision made, I started to think about the very premise of the missed approach. Airline transport pilot standards – what you needed to demonstrate to earn the highest level of U.S. pilot's license – dictated that you had to keep the azimuth needle to within ½ of its deflection from centered, commonly called "1 dot" because the instrument depicted two dots either side to depict the full scale, one dot either side for half-scale. Two dots, on most instruments, came to 1.4 degrees, so an airline transport pilot had a tolerance of just 0.7 degrees. SAM Fox standards were just the width of the needle, about a fourth of a dot, or 0.28 degrees. Pretty tight. If you did that, the runway had to be beneath your wheels!

Descending into D.C. airspace it became evident that only Baltimore and Washington-Dulles were accepting a normal flow of traffic. Washington-National was below minimums and Andrews was "at minimums," with the SAM Fox quotation marks added. As the autopilot turned us onto the ILS final approach I fired it from its appointed duties and centered the needles the old fashioned way, with stick and rudder. As the glideslope centered I gestured to Katz with my right hand, a thumbs up swiveled to the down direction. He pushed the gear handle down. After the three green lights announced our wheels were safely locked beneath us, I raised my right hand with the thumb underneath the four fingers in a flat plane, parallel to the earth. I extended my thumb downward. Katz extended the rest of our flaps. The only chatter would be to announce any deviations from perfection. We expected the horizontal and vertical indications to be within a needle width of centered. Our idea of perfection didn't include the speed, which was set to please the schedule before aerodynamics.

"A hundred to go, centered, nothing" Katz said as we passed 200 feet above the runway. We had ten seconds before minimums. I hovered my right thumb over the switch on the left side of the throttles. It would activate the "TOGA" mode of our flight director, bringing two needles into view on the flight director designed to help the pilot take off or go around. The altimeter continued unwinding.

"Minimums," Katz said. I looked up and saw nothing. The winds were calm so the runway should have been right in front of me. I started to push on the throttles, but did not press the TOGA button.

"I got a light," Katz said. Not enough, I thought and smashed the TOGA button. "Two lights," he said. "Runway."

Sure enough, there it was, right in front of us. Exactly in front of us. I ignored the TOGA commands and landed the airplane. Turning off the runway and onto the taxiways was an even bigger challenge. "I can't see enough to taxi at a normal speed," I said. "I'm going to be crawling."

"Do whatever you need to, Eddie." Katz toggled another button on his interphone panel but I couldn't follow suit, my hands and eyes were occupied with not hitting anything.

"Air Force One," I heard Katz say into his microphone, "SAM forty-nine is down. Ceiling was fifty feet and visibility just at a thousand feet." There was a pause, "It was Haskel." Another pause. "I'll pass that to him."

"His royal highness says good job, Eddie." Katz started to hum. "I've never heard him say a nice thing about one of us mortals before."

The next morning I was sitting in the left seat of an airplane headed for Europe. In the right seat was my old squadron mate and fellow non-instructor pilot Steve Kowalski. I was the official aircraft commander and the airplane was ready to go. We had the day's most important passenger and our airplane was parked in "Spot One," right in front of the passenger terminal with the red carpet leading the way to our air stairs.

"Show?" the radio operator asked.

"Call it in," I said.

Show time was our slang for being officially ready for the show. Our rulebook said we had to be ready no later than 30 minutes prior to the scheduled departure time. Being ready meant the airplane was fueled and stocked, all crewmembers in place, everything ready to put on the show. I had my prescription sunglasses perched on the nose wheel steering tiller, ready to don once the passengers were on board and the engines started. Greeting the passengers with sunglasses was strictly verboten. My regular eyeglasses were still in their case, in a cubbyhole to my left.

"Who's that colonel in the bushes?" Steve asked. He was looking across the cockpit towards the passenger lounge. I could see a figure but I wasn't sure. I put on my sunglasses.

"That's the new operations group commander," I said. "I recognize him from the base paper. He takes over next week."

"What's he doing in the bushes?" Steve asked.

"Limos on the ramp," the flight engineer announced. We dropped all talk about the nature-loving colonel and got on with the business of flying. In just a few minutes both engines were started and we were headed east. After our fuel stop at Gander, Newfoundland, we swapped seats and Steve flew us across the pond. In no time flat the English Channel was behind us.

"Steve," I said as he pulled the throttles for our initial descent into Paris, "you are thirty seconds early."

He laughed. "Are you serious?"

"Just thought you would like to know."

"If we make it within a minute we'll be fine," he said. "Nobody cares about the plus or minus five seconds except the SAM Mafia. The radio operator will report our block time to the nearest minute, so why should I care about 30 seconds?"

"Practice?" I half-asked, half-stated. Steve ignored me and landed the airplane a little early, blocked in a little early, and beamed his goofy smile. As the stairs hit the red carpet the countdown timer still had 45 seconds to go. For the next week each of Steve's block times were plus or minus no more than a minute and the radio operator dutifully reported we were on time. For each of my arrivals the countdown timer flashed "00:00" as the stairs touched.

"You are starting to get on my nerves," Steve said. I took it as a compliment. "Is it true you did a smooth missed approach last week?"

"Of course not," I said.

A week later we were back at Andrews, attending yet another change of command ceremony. The new commander of the 89th Operations Group, Colonel William Paulson, was having a few choice words about customer service.

"When Paul Paulson takes on a new mission," he started, "Paul Paulson becomes an expert in that mission."

"Who is Paul Paulson?" I heard from behind me in the audience. "I thought his name was William."

"And our mission here is serving our nation's leadership," Paulson continued.

"When the VIP in question pulls up to the airplane, everything has to be ready. The airplane has to be ready, the ground crew has to be ready, and the aircrew has to be ready. Everyone looking his or her military best! So Paul Paulson isn't in the business of chopping off heads. But let me tell you this, the next pilot I see wearing sunglasses when the VIP shows up, well, that pilot is fired!"

"Eddie," I heard from behind me, "he's looking right at you!"

The new Operations Group Commander finished his remarks and we all adjourned to the reception in his honor. I filed into the receiving line. The chief of current operations filed in behind me.

"Eddie," Stephen Jenkins said, "I have news."

"What kind of news?" I asked.

"Promotion news, of course," he said. "I have the complete list now. There are ten in the 89th Airlift Wing competing for lieutenant colonel next round. I figure you and I got it made. But we got to watch out for the shoe clerks."

It was the favorite pejorative of late. The official term was "non-rated officers." But amongst some pilots and navigators – rated officers – they were no better than shoe clerks.

"I thought you were convinced I wasn't getting promoted," I said.

"Nah," he said. "I heard about your smooth missed approach. I guess you have SAM Fox in you after all."

"I didn't do a smooth missed approach," I said.

"Then how did you land with only a thousand feet visibility?" He asked. But it wasn't really a question.

"Superior airmanship," I said.

Once I made it to the front of the line I extended my hand to grasp the colonel's outreached hand. "Major Eddie Haskel," I said, "Gulfstream aircraft commander."

"I know all about you Major," he said. "We'll have lots of time to get to know each other." With that, he turned to Jenkins. I left that line for the shrimp cocktail line, ate two shrimp, and went home.

I walked out of the house in my bare feet, clutching a pair of running shoes in one hand and socks in the other. *Number One Son* was pushing *The Little Princess* on her tricycle around and around in the driveway. Soon she wouldn't need the push.

"Daddy!" she yelled, running from the trike to me. "I can tie your shoe laces, Daddy!"

I sat as she fumbled with the laces. "Rats!" she would say with each failed attempt. She's only three, I thought. *Number One Son* didn't even make the attempt until he was four.

"Try this," I said. "First let's make a tree, starting with the roots." I helped her loop the laces over each other. "Now we put up the tree." I helped her take one of the laces into a vertical loop. "Now we make a bunny rabbit." I looped the other lace horizontally. "The bunny runs round the tree." I pulled the second loop around the first.

"Oh no! The bunny spotted you!" *The Little Princess* chortled with the glee only a three-year old can pull off. "The bunny hops into the hole." I pushed the second loop into the base of the first.

"The bunny escapes!" I pulled the two loops and the laces were tied.

"My turn!" she said. For the next ten minutes we repeated the exercise. "I hope I can remember!" she said.

"Your fingers will do the remembering," I said. "This is called muscle memory, just keep practicing and pretty soon you don't even have to think about it."

"Look, Mommy!"

I turned around to spot *The Lovely Mrs. Haskel* who had been standing behind us for quite some time.

"Some day she is going to think back on all you have taught her," *The Lovely Mrs. Haskel* said, "and think how lucky she is to have such a smart dad."

"He can have his moments," I said.

"Fewer than he thinks," she said, turning and retreating to the house. It may have been the first time she had ever insulted me. I knew asking, "What?" would only get a "Nothing" in response. Her intuition was always right, but I could only guess at what I had done to deserve her disapproval.

Normalization of Deviance

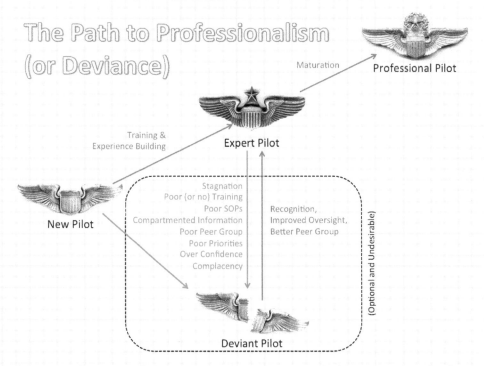

The Path to Professionalism (or Deviance)

The normalization of deviance is the incremental change to standards we once thought inviolate, turning actions once thought to be unacceptable into the new norm. The path to normalizing deviance can be paved by the lack of proper training, an experience-based ego, or expertise-based over-confidence. The ease at which one slides into the normalization of deviance can be facilitated by "group think," the lack of oversight, or a poor peer group.

Case Study: Space Shuttle Challenger, STS-51-L

The term "normalization of deviance" was coined by sociology professor Diane Vaughn in her 1996 book, The Challenger Launch Decision: Risky Technology, Culture, and Deviance at NASA, where she examines the tragedy of the 1986 launch of the Space Shuttle Challenger. A little over a minute after launch, the seals between one of the joints in one of the Solid Rocket Boosters (SRBs) permitted rocket gases to escape, cut into a spar and then the main tank. The main tank exploded seconds later, killing everyone on board.

The initial failure point was a set of O-rings in the joints which were designed to be redundant. The manufacturer of the joint stated the O-rings were

117

not reliable below 53°F, even though the initial design specification for all shuttle launch components was from 33°F to 99°F. Over the course of the shuttle's history NASA was experiencing ever increasing O-ring "blow by," especially at colder temperatures to the point they waived the redundancy requirement. As they gained experience with the Shuttle at colder and colder temperatures the minimum temperature was gradually lowered, to the point the Challenger's last launch was made at 36°F.

While early reports made it appear high level managers were violating launch rules, Professor Vaughn's work makes clear they were actually following rules that allowed these waivers. Experts believed they had the knowledge needed to justify the colder launch criteria. Information was segregated to the point where senior level managers were unaware of the O-ring temperature restrictions. NASA priorities placed the need to increase the number of launches to move the shuttle program from a "test" to an "operational" stage, as well as the need to use the cheapest possible providers of the SRB, above the need to guarantee launch safety.

You might argue that flying airplanes isn't rocket science, but many of the issues that normalized deviance at NASA exist on a day-to-day basis with many business and commercial aviation flight departments.

ISSUES

Stagnation. Flying can be an expensive hobby and at the point the money runs out amateurs find themselves with no future dreams to chase. For professionals there may also come a time when there are no further ratings to achieve and the prospects of a new career chapter seems unlikely. In either case, pilots risk a mental stagnation that weakens any motivation to keep in the books or keep up with the latest and greatest techniques and procedures.

Training. Your training is only as good as the instructor and you can be trained to deviate. This most often occurs when someone you respect who has already given in to deviant behavior assumes the role of instructor. It can also occur when a professional training vendor has misguided ideas of what should and should not be taught.

Standard Operating Procedures. We often find ourselves having to adjust, reorder, or even skip some SOPs because they don't fit the situation at hand, they would take more time than a widely accepted short cut, or we think we have a better method. Operating ad hoc, in the heat of the moment, we risk not carefully considering all possible factors, we risk forgetting something important, and crew resource management becomes more difficult as others have to guess about our actions. Once we've violated the first SOP, it becomes easier to violate the second, and the third. Before too long the culture of having SOPs will erode and when that happens, all SOPs become optional.

Compartmented Information. Pilots tend to compartmentalize information for a variety of reasons. Keeping a particular airplane's procedures separate from others, for example, can help keep cockpit procedures straight. We might want to insulate upper management from the nuts and bolts of what we do, reasoning that it is either too complicated to explain or uninteresting to non-practitioners. Some pilots may even wish to keep things quiet for fear that their ignorance on some obscure topic could be revealed. This "de facto secrecy" reduces the number of eyes available to catch deviations.

Peer Groups. Of course no professional pilot sets out to bend the rules on the margins or flagrantly disobey all SOPs; but many end up doing just that. Good pilots can be corrupted by poor peer groups. If everyone else has already normalized deviant behavior, it will seem an impossible task to hold true to SOPs without upsetting the status quo.

Priorities. When extensive training and vast experience earn us "expert" status, our non-pilot peers start to trust our judgement without question. We can be tempted to believe in our own infallability so that we place schedule, economy, and other priorities over the safe operation of our aircraft.

Over Confidence. A highly trained, highly experienced, and highly praised pilot is more likely to deviate from SOPs than a novice because of a high level of self-confidence. Ironically, the novice may exhibit safer tendencies because of an abundance of caution.

Complacency. Pilots who become comfortable with their day-to-day cockpit existence can be tempted to stop reading checklists and rely on memory, to stop taking precautions that never seemed necessary before, to start taking the "easy way" over the "right way." Highly experienced pilots and pilots in managerial positions are at greater risk because they are less likely to receive needed oversight.

SOLUTIONS

Recognition. There are ways to avoid the decline into the normalization of deviance and to recover should you find yourself in this "deviant" state. But the decline will have been gradual and with each step you will have accepted your new condition as the new normal. Recognition will be difficult.

If you ever find yourself tempted to explain the reason a short cut or improvised procedure is okay to a colleague with the phrase "I'm better than most pilots," you are probably at risk. If you've ever completed a flight without formally accomplishing any checklists, you are probably at risk. If you haven't attended any training sessions of any kind in over a year, you may be at risk. If you are reluctant to talk about aviation with pilots outside your inner circle, you might be trying to hide ignorance and could be at risk. If you've developed a reputation for always getting the job done, always beating the schedule, never cancelling a trip or never failing to arrive at the intended destination, you may be at risk. The normalization of deviance is like a cancer, but there are cures.

Stagnation. The best way to cure pilot stagnation is to realize just how challenging and exciting the profession really is and to always have a goal in sight. Even those pilots without the next rating or airplane on the horizon can motivate themselves to teach others, to write, to speak, or to mentor the next generation of pilots.

Training. If you aren't getting enough training you should let your organization's leadership know. If money or schedule are tight, the answer could be an emphatic "no." But not all training has to be formalized and provided by a vendor. There are many on-line courses. You can also organize training taught by local pilots.

Standard Operating Procedures. Any pilot who is tempted to deviate from an SOP should first think about measures to formally change the SOP. There is a definite art to this. You need to carefully analyze the existing SOP, try to understand why the SOP is constructed as it is, come up with an alternative solution, gather support from peers, and advocate the change to those who have the power to change things. Flight department leaders should work with crews to ensure that each SOP is pertinent, easily understood, easily followed, and consistent with other SOPs in the flight department and aircraft fleet. If adjustments are needed, select a well respected team member to spearhead the effort, institute a test phase, and obtain manufacturer comments if possible.

Compartmented Information. We should learn to incorporate all members of the flight department into decision making and outside expertise in fact finding. We need to understand that while getting outside counsel may momentarily make us look less than perfect, it may prevent a mistake that ends up as the headline in the next aviation news magazine. Leadership should also encourage a free flow of information laterally between crews and vertically between crews and management. Monthly meetings seem to work best, but meetings should be held at least quarterly. Think of these meetings as planned entertainment, they need to be interesting and informative if you hope to encourage the open exchange of ideas. Even if you can't include everyone because of schedule constraints, a one-page summary of the meeting can keep everyone involved.

Peer Groups. If you find yourself in an organization that has accepted the normalization of deviance you have several options. The first of which is to lead by example. Use SOPs and best practices whenever you can and when asked, provide a compelling case for the SOP.

If a senior member of the flight department insists on a non-standard procedure, ask for the reasons behind the procedure "to better understand how to accomplish the procedure." Having to verbalize the rationale may force a reexamination of the entire thought process.

If it is possible to demonstrate the efficacy of an SOP against a deviation, attempt to convince your peers to participate. If your peers are making frequent errors while flowing a checklist, for example, you can ask for a test period comparing "Do-Verify" versus "Challenge-Do-Verify," timing each and recording error rates. The results can be surprising.

It could very well be that a majority of pilots in your flight department have the same issues with some nonstandard procedures and a group meeting to discuss the issues can solve the problem. You should obtain leadership buy-in first. Leadership may be surprised about the issue; you might be surprised how open to change they can be.

It is easy to fall into nonstandard behavior without an occasional look from someone outside the flight department. If the entire organization normalizes deviance at about the same rate, no one will notice because they are all involved. You should request an outside audit, anonymous interviews, and a Line Operation Observation (LOO). An LOO should be flown on a typical trip to observe pilots in their day-to-day mode of operations. A skilled LOO pilot can determine if SOPs are an integral part of your operation.

Once you have at least two members of the flight department willing to crusade for stricter adherence to SOPs, you have what you need to apply positive peer pressure to the rest of the organization. You may be surprised that a few voices speaking as one can have powerful results. Most pilots will be alarmed to find they have become part of the problem and will welcome a wake up call.

Finally, if you have any personnel turnover you should encourage frank feedback from exit interviews. The company's human resources department or an outside auditor can accomplish this important function to gather critical data points about the health or pathology of the flight department.

[Report to the Presidential Commission on the Space Shuttle Challenger Accident, June 6th, 1986, Washington, D.C.]

[Vaughn, Dianne, The Challenger Launch Decision: Risky Technology, Culture, and Deviance at NASA, The University of Chicago Press, Chicago and London, 1996.]

[Items in blue are my comments.]

8: Deviant

C-20B landing in Lancaster, Pennsylvania (Bill Shull)

The vast majority of all 89th missions leaving Andrews were crewed by two aircraft commanders. All trips with copilots included an instructor pilot and all those trips had serious instructing going on. As a new aircraft commander, my typical month included a trip or two each week and a training flight or two each month. The trips had become fun.

I felt an instant kinship with Lieutenant Colonel Hank Richards from the day he befriended me when I walked in as the newest pilot. As I progressed on my accelerated path to this day, I looked forward to the day we could fly together. At last I had my chance. It would be the perfect trip to get to know him, to Las Vegas and back with three days off on The Strip.

I did my best to be the world's most competent copilot in the right seat as he pointed the airplane's nose to the west. After we leveled off I updated our fuel and timing computations and reported that we should arrive on time and with the predicted fuel.

"Good," he said.

I looked around the cockpit for anything amiss. There was nothing. I pulled out the approach plates for Las Vegas, compared the predicted weather to the runway alignment, and shuffled the order of the plates. "Landing to the west,"

I said. "I got those plates on top."

"A bit early to worry about that," he said.

I started to think of something else to say but was rescued by the Washington Center Air Route Traffic Control Center who wished us a pleasant day and gave us the frequency for the Indianapolis Center. In a minute I was done with my radio chores and looked to my left to see Hank studying the "Field and Stream" bow hunting special. A magazine!

I scanned the engine instruments again. On day number one in Air Force pilot training, instructor number one schooled us to check the engine instruments every fifteen minutes. For twelve years, every fifteen minutes, I checked the engine instruments. "We have a twenty PSI difference in oil pressures," I said, pointing to the round dials. "At what point does the bypass valve open?"

Hank looked up from his magazine and lifted an eyebrow. I waited for the answer, wondering if he remembered the answer in our manual was in error and that we knew the right number from the Rolls-Royce engine manual.

"I don't know," he said. "And, I don't care."

"Eggs over hard for the colonel," the flight attendant said while handing Hank a tray of breakfast. "And over easy for the major," she added while handing another tray to me. I left the systems quiz aside and split my attention between the meal and my radio chores. With each passing fifteen minutes I recomputed our timing and fuel and reported the results.

"Good," Hank said.

We repeated the cycle for the next hour until Hank finished his magazine. "Do you know why it takes less pull to hold a compound bow than to pull it in the first place?" he asked.

"The pulleys are off center," I said, extracting the information from my high school archery years.

"Explain," he said.

So for the next three hours, until it was time to begin our descent, we talked archery. Hank returned to his happy self as long as I stayed away from the subject of what we were actually doing, flying the United States Secretary of State in a hollow aluminum tube at eight-tenths the speed of sound. Once we began our descent, however, he returned to the task at hand.

"Plus five on the box," he said, "behind thirty seconds."

"Checks," I said. Our flight management system didn't understand the decay of true airspeed with altitude and we had to add five minutes to its estimated time of arrival when we were between 50 and 60 nautical miles from the airport. He would be doing this mental math continuously until we shut the engines down and I would parallel his efforts, speaking up only when our arithmetic differed. But it didn't and we arrived in front of the local news station about 15 seconds late. Not up to SAM Fox standards, but good enough for the radio operator to report "on time."

The flight engineer, flight attendant, and radio operator devoted themselves to poker and Keno for the next three days. Hank favored black jack on the dollar tables and I dutifully followed along after memorizing a book of percentages. We both decided we needed another activity after the first time I criticized his play.

"You have a better than even chance of busting if you hit on a fourteen or higher," I offered, helpfully of course. "The dealer's highest chance of busting is with a five showing. You should have stayed."

"Eddie," he said. "I don't mean to offend you. But shut the hell up."

I shut the hell up. That night we learned our commander in chief was losing his job and our beloved Timberwolf would be replaced on January 20th. Hank and I walked the length of Las Vegas Boulevard while cataloging all the faults of the new boss, of which there were many.

"Who was the last President with no military experience?" Hank asked. I thought for a moment. Bush, Carter, Nixon, Johnson, Kennedy were all Navy. Reagan was in the Army Air Force, of course. And then there was Eisenhower and Truman, both in the Army.

"FDR," I guessed.

"Damned straight," he said. "And how many commanders in chief did we have who dodged the draft?"

I let the question drop. While politics was rarely a good topic of discussion for any flight crew, it was easy to predict how our officer corps felt about the next boss. "You hear his call sign yet?" Hank asked.

"Yeah."

During the campaign the Secret Service call signs for each candidate revealed the next focus of our Air Force One and back up trips: "Eagle."

"Should have been 'Dodger' if you ask me," he said.

Our passengers were a bit hung over during the flight back and the flight attendant spent most her time in the cockpit, trading stories with Hank and the flight engineer. I kept to myself in the left seat, worrying over the flight plan, our tailwind, and the block time to come back at Andrews. That was the last place on planet earth where blowing an ETA could be overlooked.

"Two minutes early," I announced, "pulling it back point oh oh five."

Hank wrinkled his brow, diverted his eyes for a second, and returned to the joke in progress. The flight attendant issued her customary giggle. Memphis Center asked us to contact the next air traffic control sector.

"Hey get that for me, Eddie." Hank returned to the conversation just aft of the airplane's two front seats. After an hour the flight attendant decided it was time to start the next meal and the cockpit fell silent again. I tilted my head back against the headrest and started to think about direct current generators and the efficiency of converting those electrons to alternating current and back again. Our Gulfstream's engines produced a very unstable form of DC power, converted that to stable AC, and then to stable DC for all the airplane's electronics. The gauges were not as stable as advertised.

"You ever notice," I said while pointing to the overhead AC and DC gauges.

"Eddie," Hank said, cutting me off mid-sentence. "I like you and whenever we talk about anything other than the damned airplane you are a lot of fun. But I don't want to talk about airplanes. Especially not when I'm flying one."

That makes no sense at all, I thought to myself.

"We got three kinds of pilots," he continued. "You need to decide which kind of pilot you want to be. First, we got the Mafia pilots. These are the instructors dreaming about being the President's pilot and trying to outdo all the other Mafia pilots along the way. Second, we got everyone who wants to get elevated into the Mafia. These are copilots and aircraft commanders trying to become instructors. And then we got people like me. We don't have a shot in hell at being invited into the Mafia. So we play the game whenever we fly a training flight with an instructor or have to fly a trip with a Mafia pilot. But when we get turned loose without the Mafia, we fly by our own rules and don't play a hundred questions at altitude. So you gotta decide what kind of pilot you want to be, Eddie."

Two months later Timberwolf was gone and Eagle took over. Eagle's First Lady announced they would not be using that huge waste of taxpayer dollars at Andrews Air Force Base and the news media happily followed her from the White House to Washington National where she boarded an airliner with a hundred other passengers on her way to a secret meeting about health care. We watched the news reports with envy and fear.

"What if they never fly us?" I asked while perched in front of the empty SAM Fox current operations board.

"They'll figure it out," Major Stephen Jenkins said. "They always do."

Jenkins explained that one of his clerks had been in the office since the Carter days. "The Republicans take office, nothing changes until the Democrats start talking about the abuse of power, and then the flying decreases. The Democrats take power and all flying stops, until they figure out the Air Force pays for it, and then we start flying even more than before."

I had to wonder. For the next two months we flew only training sorties. In May the White House travel office was fired and I flew my first trip in months. Our passenger was the First Lady. A week later our first Congressional trip was scheduled and within a month we were flying at almost double the Republican rate. The drought was over.

"Don't forget," Bobby said from the right seat, "he only wants Chicago time."

I nodded. It was a ritual played out in every SAM Fox cockpit. The aircraft commander had to handwrite a note for the lead passenger relating the weather at the destination and the ETA in the local time zone. We were stopping at Gander International Airport, Newfoundland, Canada for fuel on our way to Warsaw, Poland. In the summertime Andrews was at Greenwich Mean Time minus 4, or GMT-4. Gander was at GMT-3. Chicago was GMT-5. I made the conversion, signed the blue card, and handed it to Captain Bobby Fielding. "Looks good," he said, and handed it to our flight attendant, waiting behind the flight engineer.

Bobby was hired at Andrews two years earlier than me, upgraded about the same time, but assumed his role as my copilot without complaint. While rank was supposedly unimportant in any SAM Fox squadron, most of the captains paid the appropriate level of military respect to majors and other officers of higher rank.

"Weather is pretty close to minimums," he said after listening to the airport's automated weather system. "The alternate is okay."

"Thanks," I said. In a sane world we would simply head for the alternate when the destination was only needed for fuel. But our rules were less than sane and the prestige and reputation of the 89th Airlift Wing depended on us achieving our stated schedule. "We'll be fine."

"On time," he reported as I turned the airplane to align with the instrument landing system on the airport's northerly runway. The aircraft was a bit heavy but the winds were light and the course needle behaved itself. Bobby was silent except for checklist items. "A thousand feet above minimums, gear is down, flaps are set."

"Winds are calm," Gander tower offered without us asking. "Visibility is twenty six hundred feet, you are cleared to land. Last airplane landed thirty minutes ago and reported a ceiling of two hundred feet."

Bobby acknowledged.

I pulled my eyes away from the instruments just long enough to look at the minima box on the approach plate. Our minimum was 2,600 feet, or a half a mile of visibility. Good enough.

"Five hundred above," Bobby said. "Nothing yet."

The needles would have to be centered in weather like this. I had half of a needle width's deviation on the azimuth and gave the ailerons a quick wiggle. Centered.

"Two hundred above," Bobby said. "Nothing yet."

I thought about that word, "yet." It wasn't a part of the required call out, but it made grammatical sense. He didn't see the runway. Yet. The needles were centered, not so much as the width of a human hair between the needle and its reference mark. So if one needle-width is 0.28 degrees, no needle-widths are . . ."

"One hundred above. Nothing yet."

The needles stayed centered and our airspeed was just a few knots high. The vertical velocity indicator showed us descending at 650 feet per minute. So another hundred feet would take . . .

"Minimums," he said in a more forceful tone. "Negative contact, go around."

I toggled the flight director's go around button, nudged the throttles forward, and looked up. "I see two lights," I said. "Do you agree?"

"Yes."

I pulled the throttles back and landed the airplane.

Our passengers got up to visit the Gander fixed base operator's snack bar in an effort to stretch their legs and to be able to say they had actually been to Newfoundland. The Chairman of the House Ways and Means Committee was last to leave, stopping at the cockpit first.

"Son," he said while patting my right shoulder. "That was a mighty fine landing. I'm gonna go inside to take a leak and maybe get some ice cream. But when I come back I want you to explain to me exactly how you did that."

"Yes, sir." I smiled and he left.

"I wonder what all that is about," I said, to no one in particular.

"It was pretty amazing," the flight attendant said from behind me. "From the cabin we never saw the runway or any lights at all until you pulled off the runway."

I busied myself with programming the flight computers with the next flight plan and thought about the Chairman's comment. It would make a good war story, that.

"That was pretty neat," Bobby said from the right seat. "I've heard about the smooth missed approach before, but never saw it in action. I hope to learn the secret to that someday, sir."

"That wasn't a smooth missed approach," I said.

"Yes, sir."

We finished reprogramming the computers and reorganizing our charts, approach plates, and logs. The engineer would be a few more minutes paying the bills and we had the cockpit to ourselves to swap seats. Bobby would fly us to Warsaw and I would assume the role of dutiful copilot. The Chairman forgot about his promised question and I was left to ponder the smooth missed approach. It was the second time I had been accused of such aviation heresy and SAM Fox folklore. It is a fundamental of pilot instrument procedure: you execute a missed approach if you don't see the runway at minimums. But I saw the runway.

"Pilot, radio," we heard over the interphone.

"Go ahead," Bobby said.

"Air Force Two on button two," he said. Bobby looked at me. He was in the pilot position but I was the trip's aircraft commander. I reached down and pushed the second button on the third row of our interphone panel.

"Air Force Two," I said, "this is SAM six oh two pilot."

"Ah yeah," I heard in response. "This is Lieutenant Colonel Clevis Haney, Air Force Two pilot. Our Warsaw ETA is the same as yours. We're gonna push it up to gain five, but we need you to pull it back to lose ten."

"Wilco," I said.

Air Force Two is a "code two" in the hierarchy of Very Important Persons, at least in the eyes of the U.S. military. Any head of state is automatically a code one. Our passenger was a code four. We could not arrive sooner than fifteen minutes after the code two, in order to give the Vice President ample time for the pomp and circumstance surely headed his way.

"Add ten to our blocks," I said to the radio operator.

"Already done," he said.

"What kind of name is Clevis for a SAM pilot?" I asked the ether.

"He's a legend," Bobby said. "A friend of mine in the other squadron says he's bullet proof for some reason. The more he screws up, the better off he becomes." Bobby explained that Clevis was hired at the 89th to fly the C-12 King Air turboprop. That's where all the pilots that were on the bottom of each new hire list were sent for further seasoning and evaluation. Those that survived were promoted to jets, those that didn't, stayed in the King Air until it was time to leave the 89th. Clevis had the good sense to get promoted to lieutenant colonel while flying the King Air, and the 89th had no choice but to give him the jet.

"He's not too sharp so they usually pair him with a strong crew," Bobby said.

"Amazing," I said. "I know that goes on in the mortal Air Force. I thought we were immune to that at the 89th."

"Guess not," Bobby said.

A few hours later we were on schedule for our new ETA and we had the weather for Warsaw. "Weather is good," I said from the right seat. "Five kilometers and light rain, the ILS needs only seven hundred fifty meters."

Bobby studied his ILS approach plate and I dialed in the necessary radio frequencies. The Instrument Landing System was the best thing going for any instrument pilot. Once you had those needles centered, the only thing you had to worry about was if your decision altitude would be measured in feet or meters above the runway or above mean sea level. At Warsaw it was feet and above mean sea level.

Just prior to starting our descent the automated weather frequency came to life. I listened and realized our plan had to be changed. "ILS is out of service," I said to Bobby. "Expect the VOR to runway eleven."

We both flipped through our approach plates and studied. The VOR, a VHF Omnidirectional Range transmitter, put out navigation signals that were not quite as accurate as the ILS and required that we descend to a Minimum Descent Altitude (MDA) before looking for the runway. Once we spotted the runway we could descend, but before that the MDA was as low as we could go. The standard technique was to "dive" from the final approach fix altitude down to the MDA, and then "drive" at that altitude until the runway was in sight.

"You notice anything strange about this approach?" I asked.

"Yeah, that's a real long final approach."

"Eight miles is pretty close to the limit," I said. "Why don't you figure us a VDP and I'll do the same."

Aviation history is littered with the carcasses of airplane after airplane where the dive and drive ended badly. While these so-called "non-precision" approaches had been around since the dawn of instrument flight, we had only recently learned to figure a visual descent point, or VDP, as the best way to figure out the optimal time to leave the MDA. If you spotted the runway before the VDP, you waited. If you spotted the runway after the VDP, it was probably too late to land so you would go around.

Figuring a VDP is easy. You subtract the runway's touchdown zone elevation from the MDA to get the height above touchdown. You then divide that by altitude lost every nautical mile in a 3 degree glide path, which is 318 feet. We had an MDA of 800 feet and a touchdown zone elevation of 362 feet.

"One point four," Bobby said.

"That's what I got," I said. The radio beacon was 0.5 nautical miles down the end of the runway so we had a VDP of 1.4 + 0.5 = 1.9 nautical miles.

Ten minutes later we were on the approach, at 3,000 feet, getting ready for the "dive" to the MDA. Warsaw's radar was out and they asked for an "established" call, which I gave.

"SAM Six Oh Two," the controller responded. "You are cleared for the VOR Runway One One approach. Be advised Polish Regulations require all aircraft remain at or above a normal glide path until landing."

"Copy," I said. "It is the same in the United States."

"Well, please do advise your colleagues then."

"Wilco."

Bobby gave me a "what the heck?" look. I shrugged. With 8.6 nautical miles to go, Bobby pulled both throttles back and adjusted the aircraft's pitch. I watched as the altimeter unwound and Bobby reversed his inputs so as to leave the airplane level at 800 feet, our MDA. "Runway in sight," I said about three miles out. "Another mile before your VDP."

"Roger," he said. A minute later, as the distance meter read 1.9, he pulled both throttles. "Departing MDA, landing flaps please."

The rain had picked up considerably, but we landed and pulled off the runway. The rain intensified. "Timing is everything," I said. Bobby followed the florescent yellow "Follow Me" truck, which we could barely make out in the rain-turned-monsoon. After we blocked in, the flight engineer opened the aircraft door and handed each passenger an umbrella for his or her mad dash to the waiting vans.

I busied myself with paperwork, the flight engineer donned rain gear for the exterior work, and the rest of the crew worked on getting the cabin presentable for the next flight. As the rain finally let up I could see the unmistakable silhouette of a Boeing 707 parked right in front of us.

"Aircraft is ready for bed," the flight engineer said after returning to the cockpit. "Airport boys say our van will be here as soon as the Vice President leaves."

"What?"

We looked forward to the Boeing 707. The rain was down to a sprinkle and we could finally see the unmistakable colors of the 89th Airlift Wing aircraft. To the right was a procession of vehicles and people standing in the rain. At the head of the procession was the man who earned the Nobel Peace Prize in 1983, helped bring down the Iron Curtain in 1987, and became the President of Poland in 1990. He appeared to be drenched.

I punched the radio panel for our common frequency. "Air Force Two, this is SAM six oh two."

"Go ahead." It was that same Kentucky drawl from our earlier call.

"Clevis," I said, "did you know President Walesa is standing off your right wing, soaked to the bone?"

"Yeah," he said. "I know. What in the hell can I do about it? We told our pax, but they don't want to leave the airplane until the rain lets up. Wait, no. Here they go."

The frequency went dead and we saw the Vice President of the United States leave the airplane, as dry as could be. He shook the wet President's hand and in a few minutes they were all gone.

That night at the hotel bar I finally got my chance to meet the legend, Lieutenant Colonel Clevis Haney. I spotted his cowboy boots right off and guessed. "Clevis?"

"Yeah that's me," he said.

"Eddie Haskel," I said, "from SAM Six Oh Two."

"Howdy," he said, putting down his beer and tipping an imaginary hat our way. Bobby and I took the two seats to his right and ordered our own beers.

Clevis seemed to have a hybrid Kentucky accent, not quite southern but not Appalachian either. His thin, blond hair betrayed a scalp littered with freckles, which provided the needed complement to a face, pockmarked through teenaged acne. But those teenage years had to have been decades in the past.

"So how's things in the little plane?" he asked.

"Things are good," I said. "Hey, did you guys get that strange call from tower about staying above the glide path?"

"Nah," he said, "but they should'a said something. That runway's got some kinda visual thing going on. You can hardly tell where the runway begins and the not-runway ends."

"Yeah, I suppose." I said. "The final approach segment is longer than most. We computed a VDP just to be sure."

"VDP?" he said. "There was no damned VDP on that approach."

"That's right," I said. "So we computed our own."

"Sounds like witchcraft to me, son." Clevis tired of my company and turned in his seat to the next person over. It seemed he was more interested in talking to somebody else. Anybody else.

Bobby shook his head and whispered, "I'm surprised he doesn't know that, we did that routinely in the C-141."

"The concept of a visual descent point is pretty new," I said.

"I guess '*experto crede*' isn't all it is cracked up to be," Bobby said.

The next day we left Warsaw for a few other Polish cities and left Air Force Two and Clevis behind. A week later we were home again.

"You did another smooth missed approach?" Steve Kowalski asked. The inflection in his voice betrayed that the question was more of an accusation. We were in the training office, his turf and my normal refuge from the madness of the Operations Group Headquarters. I wasn't expecting the verbal assault.

"Of course not," I said.

"Bobby says he called for the go around and you gently pushed the throttles forward," Steve said. "Of course he was bragging about it to anyone who would listen and the SAM Mafia was eating it up. You're a hero, Eddie."

"Nonsense," I said. "Besides, flying the needle centered changes things, doesn't it? Did you know a needle width comes to just zero point two eight degrees!"

"What's that come to in feet?" he asked.

"I don't know," I said. "Let's find out." I pulled out my pocket calculator. The lateral offset would be equal to the distance from the antenna times the trigonometric tangent of the angle. The localizer antenna is usually at the other side of the runway, which could be as long as two miles. Just to be conservative I punched into my calculator 2 times the distance of a nautical mile in feet, 6,076 feet to be exact. I multiplied that answer by the tangent of 0.28 degrees. Another one of those chills ran down my spine.

"Most runways with an ILS approach are at least 100 feet wide," Kowalski continued as I checked my math. "So you could be as much as 50 feet left or right minus half your wheel span and still be over pavement. What's our wheel span, Eddie?"

"Huh," I said.

"Our wheel span. What is it?"

"Ah," I said, "Fourteen feet."

"So if we are within 50 minus 7, or 43 feet, we are over pavement," he said. "So what does that point two eight come to?"

"Sixty feet," I said. "Not enough," I admitted.

"Besides all that," he said, pouring salt on my fresh wound, "what if your instruments aren't in perfect tune. What if the navigation aid isn't just right? Don't you engineers say error is cumulative?"

"It is," I admitted.

"Sometimes we deviate from the rules when we are convinced we've thought things through and the mission requires it," he said.

"National security," I said.

"Yeah," he said. "But after a while we just start deviating for the hell of it. It's like we've forgotten how to fly by the book." I let his words hang.

"I used to think you were a 'by-the-book' pilot, Eddie."

"I am," I said.

"You used to be," he said.

Procedural Intentional Non-Compliance

The central issue in many mishaps is "procedural intentional noncompliance," or PINC. Yes, it is true that we all make mistakes now and then; we violate procedures unintentionally. But flying a high performance aircraft in a dynamic environment isn't easy and we have safeguards built in via cockpit automation, crew resource management, and redundant procedures. These procedures are designed to protect us. When we intentionally violate procedures these safeguards break down. When we do this habitually, it is only a matter of time before it all catches up with us.

[Huntzinger] What's interesting is that PINC events typically involve crews who have been flying most of their adult lives — veteran aviators who train on simulators once or twice a year; attend initial and then recurrent training classes that cover procedures, FARs, limitations and other best practices; practice CRM; ride with check airmen; and so on. In short, they clearly know the rules and regulations, yet they intentionally violate them.

Aviators who have reached the top – the senior airline captain or the business aviation chief pilot – are at the highest risk. They know their jobs and are in positions where there is very little push back from above or below.

[Huntzinger] From research and practical experience, we have found that there are three elements to a PINC event. First, there is some sort of reward for the violator; second, it follows a situational assessment, which covers, at the very least, the associated risks; and third, the action is unlikely to produce any adverse reaction from peers. You have to have all three elements in place to go PINC. If any one of them is missing or incomplete, the whole process shuts down.

Rewards (Economic)

[Huntzinger] One of the major motivators is economic, whether it is for the person or the company served. A good example occurred a few years ago, when La Guardia Airport was hammered by a heavy, wet snowstorm. The plows and ground de-icing equipment were keeping pace and the airport was open, but most crews canceled their flights because the snowfall was so heavy they could not get from the deicing pit to the runway with a safe margin. Most crews. However, two flights departed, both from the same airline. Do you know why? That particular airline paid by the flight. That is, the pilots were not on salary, but paid by each leg completed. No fly, no pay.

"No fly, no pay" applies to a lot of airline crews who are paid by the hour unless they have provisions for trip guarantees. (They are paid even if the trip cancels.) When the crew's paycheck depends on flying, the motivation to violate a procedure is high.

Rewards (Personal)

[Huntzinger] Another reward is internally driven and has to do with a sense of duty, the "it-is-my-job-and-I'll-get-it-done" syndrome. Pride is a motivator as well. It's closely associated to duty, but not quite the same thing. Pride involves being known as the go-to guy, the one everyone counts on to get the job done. Lots of people take pride in their abilities and rightly so. Many of us are very competent at a challenging, complex profession and we like it when people recognize that fact.

When pilots have a personal relationship with passengers, there is additional pressure to ensure our positive reputations do not suffer by failing to accomplish an assigned task.

Rewards (Get-Home-itis)

[Huntzinger] The personal lives of the crew are often motivators as well. How many of us have missed a soccer game or an anniversary? How many of us have been threatened with making the next one or else?

Here again, having a personal relationship with passengers multiplies the number of cases of get-home-itis that might adversely affect a pilot's decisions.

Situational Assessment

[Huntzinger] Once a motivator has been established, there has to be some feeling that by ignoring the rules, the outcome will likely be successful. This assessment involves several considerations, or questions: Can I handle this? Do I have the skills, experience or the hardware to even do this? Can I get away with this?

The threat of being caught increases with larger organizations because there are more "witnesses" without a personal stake in the successful outcome of the procedural noncompliance. It follows, then, that the threat of being caught is decreased in small flight departments, especially those flying from small airfields.

Adverse Reaction from Peers

[Huntzinger] The last PINC element involves fellow pilots, colleagues, passengers or superiors — one's peers. A person blows off the rules only when confident that no one in the peer group will react negatively. The absence of negative reaction could result from their not knowing, from knowing and not caring, or actually endorsing the behavior. Regardless, if no one is likely to criticize or complain, think PINC.

When the top pilot is infected with PINC, the disease metastasizes; that is. it spreads like a cancer. Any chief pilot needs to worry that not only does his or her actions place the flight operation at risk, but these same actions telegraph the message to everyone else that PINC is tolerated.

Research

[Huntzinger] I have discovered that while not all PINC events end in disaster, many disasters begin with PINC episodes. That probably results from the fact that people tend to underestimate the situation and overestimate their abilities. Research back in the 1980s, Boeing did a study of 232 accidents. One of its researchers' findings was that the pilot flying (PF) failed to follow procedures in about half of the events and that the pilot monitoring (PM) failed to follow procedures in about 20 percent of the accidents. These actions combined with some other nonstandard situations involving weather, ATC, maintenance and such to cause the accident. The crews were aware of some of the nonstandard situations while they happened, but were unaware of others. The average number of contributing factors was four and the highest was 20.

Prevention (Economic)

[Huntzinger] So to prevent PINC from occurring, consider ways to counter the economic motivation, be that to benefit the individual or the individual's company. One mitigation scheme is to put crews on salary rather than paying them by the leg. If the pilot knows that they will be paid, regardless of whether the flight is completed or not, one temptation to avert the rules is removed.

Similarly, companies should build some flexibility into schedules to accommodate delays and into their cost structures to cover the costs associated with delays and thereby ease the pilots' worries and their inclination to push on when they should not.

Having a Plan B for alternate transportation or hotel accommodations pre-arranged or considered can help alleviate the inconvenience of an aborted trip or diversion. Any additional incurred costs should be considered to be an insurance policy.

[Huntzinger] To eliminate PINC, it's important to eliminate passengers from the formula. Create procedures that prevent passengers from interfering with the conduct of the flight. They can plead, rant and rave but the approach criteria, for example, are cast in concrete. If they continue to interfere, have them removed from the area and banned from flying with you in the future. This can all be preempted by having a proactive program that clearly explains to passengers their roles, responsibilities and the limits of their authority.

It helps to have senior leadership buy-in. If the CEO has a "don't interfere with the pilots" philosophy you obviously bypass many of these problems. But how do you gain this level of trust from your company's top leaders? You can do this by frequently (and accurately) framing all decisions in terms of safety. A "flow control" delay, for example, can be better explained to be a problem of "too many airplanes and too little airspace due to hazardous weather." If the senior leadership knows safety is a top concern on days where the trip does get from Point A to Point B, they will be more receptive when the trip ends up at Point C or never leaves in the first place.

Prevention (Personal)

[Huntzinger] To counter a wrongheaded sense of "duty," examine the operations culture and its ops procedures.

This is a leadership problem. We need to stop celebrating hacking the mission under impossible odds and apologizing for delays, cancellations, and diverts. In fact, we should flip those. When a crew finds itself as the only aircraft to make it off the ground during a heavy fog, we need to ensure no corners were cut. If a crew abandons an approach well before the missed approach point and ends up at the alternate, we need to celebrate their timely and safe decision-making.

Prevention (Situational Assessment)

[Huntzinger] Beyond that, there must be clear disincentives for risk-taking and PINC episodes. These could include fines, demotions, suspensions or even termination. Many companies make procedures compliance a condition of continued employment. One less drastic but powerful consequence is to make the perpetrator go out and teach people about compliance. For many pilots, speaking in public is a fate worse than death.

A word of caution here. If you uncover a PINC episode, do not jump to conclusions. Investigate and then act. There may have been a good reason why the person did PINC. There may have been an emergency. It could be that the rule is old and overcome by events and needs rework. Maybe it was an unwritten rule or the rule was inappropriate for the conditions. Be sure to understand why. And there may have been a bad reason why there was PINC. Maybe management coerced them and things turned out bad, so a scapegoat was needed. They could have been pressured by peers, a passenger or something else. Find out what it was and fix it.

A good safety program can defuse many of these problems as the anonymous reporting system gives people the opportunity to speak up, ahead of time. You will have to look for the underlying factors, just as they were described above. Always ask: Why?

Prevention (Setting a Personal Example)

The best way to prevent Procedural Intentional Noncompliance in ourselves is also the best way to prevent it in others; we should set a good "by the book" example and brag about it. By becoming vocal advocates for procedural compliance we place a personal stake in the game. If we were then to break with this philosophy, not only are we violating a procedure, we are going back on our publicly proclaimed ethics. When we hear or witness procedural intentional noncompliance, we need to speak up.

[Huntzinger, David, Ph.D., "In the PINC," Business & Commercial Aviation, January 2006]

[Items in blue are my comments.]

9: Welcome Back, Eddie!

C-20B in Faro Portugal (Pedro Aragão)

Presence. That is a quality few Air Force officers think about when they start out, but it becomes pretty obvious with any experience in the command structure. When an officer who has it enters the room, everyone knows it. It is usually associated with advanced rank or position. A general officer has it; those stars on each shoulder guarantee it. The wing commander has it; everyone on base knows it. But there are other kinds of presence.

Expertise. That is the best kind of presence. The world beats a path to the true expert's doorstep. Steve Kowalski had that in a previous life; but at Andrews he lost all that presence because he didn't have the SAM Fox Mafia's stamp of approval. But for those of us who knew him, his presence was not to be trifled with. Steve's rebuke – "You used to be a by-the-book pilot" – would hang over me for the rest of my time as a SAM Fox pilot. Steve's disapproval meant nothing to the 89th, of course. But to me it was crushing.

Fame. There are other exceptions to the rule of rank and position, of course. My next trip was with a fallen rock star who had a presence of another kind. Wherever Lieutenant Colonel Fred Spelling went, heads were turned and fingers were pointed. "There goes Thunderbird Solo." When the Air Force aerial demonstration team began its 1990 season, a ten-pound turkey vulture found its way into Fred's engine and forced him to eject at high speed. His back injuries meant he would never again sit in an ejection seat. Fred needed a home and the 89th wanted a rock star. But things didn't work out as planned.

As accomplished as Fred was in fighters, he was doing little more than occupying space in the squadron line up. He was a capable aircraft commander and an excellent pilot, but he would never be elevated to instructor pilot. He was certainly up to the task but, as the squadron put these things, "His blood pressure was found lacking." You just couldn't get Fred excited about anything.

"You made a decision yet?" I asked.

"No," he said. "I need a little more time."

We were flying the Base Realignment And Closure Committee from Washington, D.C. to Charleston, South Carolina. The BRAC Committee was given unparalleled power to close unneeded bases and was the Chamber of Commerce's worst nightmare. They had already closed hundreds of Army, Navy, and Air Force installations with ruthless efficiency. It had done wonders for the Department of Defense's bottom line. Now Charleston was in the crosshairs.

"We got to declare," I said.

"Just a minute," he said.

We had filed a flight plan from Andrews to Charleston International Airport, something sure to get the local news media's attention. We were in our unmarked airplane and had a non-SAM call sign. But that wasn't the only planned deception. It was up to Fred to pick another airport to throw the dogs off our scent, but he had to do so at least an hour before landing to give the ground transportation team a chance to get into position.

"Fred," I said, "if you don't pick an airport I will."

"Eddie," he said, "back off. Give me another minute."

It was the first time I had ever heard Fred raise his voice. "Steady Freddie" he was called. I had upset him. I decided it was time to back off.

"Pilot, radio," we heard from the crew interphone. "Andrews wants an answer and a block time."

"Charleston Executive," he said. "Standby on the block time."

I called air traffic control with our amended intentions, pulled out the charts, and programmed our flight computers. I jotted the distances and time until our descent, which was soon, and Fred scribbled a few numbers on his approach plate.

"Seventeen minutes from TOD to blocks," he said. My numbers took us to Top Of Descent so the math was done.

"Ten past," I said over the interphone. "Stairs on the ground at ten past."

Fred got us to TOD on time but the winds picked up and his 17-minute approach prediction was falling short. I ran the calculations after we got to TOD and came up with 20 minutes.

"Fred," I said, "you need to pick it up."

"I'm not flying faster than this," he said. "What else can I do?"

"Weather's good," I said. "How about we get priority clearance for a short final?"

"I don't want a short final," he said.

Fred, I decided, didn't want my help. I once again decided that I would back off. Our wheels touched down three minutes late and the airstairs touched the ground two minutes late, a minute later than SAM Fox standards.

Of course it really didn't matter. The passengers were greeted only by the limos prepositioned to whisk them away secretly. I worried the 89th would exact retribution on us both. "You ever had to call in a late block time before?" I asked the radio operator.

"All the time," he said. "The wing gets upset with some of the pilots, I know. But Colonel Spelling doesn't care and I think the 89th is okay with that. It's only guys like you that care."

"Guys like me?" I asked.

"You know, sir," he said. "The guys who play the game."

For the next five days we were ordered to keep a low profile so the enlisted crewmembers devoted themselves to cards in the flight engineer's hotel room. Fred had planned museums, botanical gardens, and civil war sites for each day.

"So why does it take so long for you to make a decision, Fred?" I asked as we strolled along another garden.

"I like to consider everything," he said.

"How did you survive supersonic speeds in the F-16?" I asked.

"At those speeds," he said, "the quicker you decide the quicker you die."

"Makes sense," I said. Fred never seemed to take offense to my direct questioning and his philosophy of flight was starting to sound familiar.

"If cutting the corner on an approach gains you a minute," he said, "but risks you not getting the needles centered before you are at obstacle height, it isn't worth it."

"Makes sense," I said again. But that's why we train so hard, I thought. For every operational hour we trained ten. We were able to cut those corners safely because we practiced doing just that. Or was that just how we convinced ourselves it was okay?

"They teach us to takeoff without a full set of systems," he continued, "and we tell ourselves we are good enough to do that. But if something goes wrong, wouldn't it have been worth the trouble to have the problem fixed first?"

"Makes sense," I said, yet again. Of course the airplane was built with redundancies. We could fly without everything in perfect working order; the airplane was designed to do just that. But we often took off with something not right just to save a few minutes. Was the block time worth the risk?

By day three it appeared we agreed on just about every aspect of flying. I was running out of questions but had avoided the one question that needed to be asked. Fred was well liked in the squadron but it was obvious to all he would never be added to the SAM Fox Mafia roster, he would never be the President's pilot, and he would never go further than a Gulfstream aircraft commander. Fred was comfortable with that. The question lingered.

On our flight home I decided to ask the unaskable. "Fred, you ever seen a smooth missed approach?"

"Once," he said. "It was Don Newsome. I called the go around and he just said 'wait.' In another fifty feet we saw the runway and landed."

"Fifty feet!" I said.

"Yeah. I told Don that the next time he did that with me I was going to beat him to death with my bare hands."

"Really?" I asked.

"Yeah," he said. "We've never flown together since."

"The list is on base," Stephen Jenkins said as I strolled into his current operations office. "It's good news for you and me."

"You've seen the list?" I asked.

"No," he said. "But I got a source in the wing commander's office. Only two pilots got promoted. Two! The rest were all shoe clerks. So that's bad news for eight SAM Fox pilots. Oh well, too bad for them, good for us."

"I heard they are going to ground pilots who don't get promoted," I said. "I know they are doing that at other bases, but I didn't think that was possible at Andrews."

"Well wake up," he said. "Andrews is becoming like the rest of the Air Force. In fact, it is worse than that. They are going to start going over each squadron's roster and throwing out guys with the most time on station. So even if you do get promoted, you can get tossed. But that doesn't matter for you and me." He got up and strolled to the window facing the current operations parking lot. "See that red convertible?"

I walked to the window and spotted the car. It was hard to miss. "Corvette?" I asked.

"Yeah," he said. "I got her as soon as I heard. Lieutenant colonels make a lot more money than majors."

"She's a good looking car," I said.

"Too bad you're going to miss the party," he said. "The list comes out tomorrow night but you're going to be in Seattle. I'll have an extra beer for you."

It was my first Air Force One back up trip with Hank Richards, my first with someone clearly not a member of the SAM Fox mafia. These weren't like the normal trips with a load of senators, ambassadors, or other dignitaries on board. Those trips were fun. The back up trip meant flying under a microscope and being tethered to the airplane during your ground time. No tourism, no beer, no nothing. But the worst part was that microscope. Any mistakes were reported instantly and the price for failure could be SAM Fox disbarment.

It would also be my first back up trip under the new White House. Since all these trips were secret, there wasn't a lot of word about what to expect; we just expected more of the same. The rules for a coast-to-coast trip would be for the

Gulfstream to takeoff as early as an hour before Air Force One, fly as fast as the timing required and the fuel would permit, and land precisely fifteen minutes after the faster Boeing. We had been doing it that way for nearly eight years, ever since the Boeing 747 first arrived wearing Presidential colors. But things were changing.

"Hold," we heard on Air Force One's private frequency. "We are delayed."

"Delayed?" Hank said from the left seat. "What the hell does delay mean?"

"Pilot," the radio operator said over the interphone, "Eagle hasn't left the White House yet. He's running late."

"Late?" Hank asked. "How is that possible?"

Indeed, that was a good question. For the previous twelve years you could set your watch to the comings and goings of Air Force One. The President was always on time, to the second. That made things easy for the back up airplane. If Air Force One was scheduled for a 1015 departure and a 1530 arrival, the backup crew knew takeoff would be at 1000 and landing would be at 1545, to the second. Now we were airborne, headed to the other side of the country, and had to hold.

I got permission from Washington Center to hold and pulled out our fuel charts. "We need to pull it back to point seven two, Hank. She's going to be sloppy at that speed."

Hank pulled the throttles back and set about trying to hold the slower speed with minimal throttle movement. Deviating from the airplane's maximum endurance speed or excessive throttle jockeying would rob us of jet fuel. We needed every drop to make it to Seattle. The flight normally took five hours and left us with an hour of extra fuel. But we had already been airborne for an hour.

"Marine One is airborne," we heard from our private frequency.

"At last!" Hank said.

"Let's head west," I said.

"We haven't been cleared yet," Hank said.

"When they clear us they are going to have us resume the speed schedule," I said. "We don't have the gas to do that."

"Yeah," Hank said. "Okay."

We got air traffic control clearance to resume our flight plan, but at a slower speed. The radio operator handed a timing sheet forward with Air Force One's new block time and our expected time, fifteen minutes later.

"What's the longest flight you ever had in a Gee Three?" I asked.

"Six point eight," Hank said. "But that was a slick bird, not one of these."

And that was the problem. The back up airplanes weighed an extra thousand pounds because of all the communications gear. That was a thousand pounds less fuel. We were flying much slower than our flight plan called for, saving fuel.

"How's the block time?" Hank asked, already knowing the answer.

"We're falling behind," I said. "Let's see how it goes, maybe we can speed up at the end. Maybe the God of Wind will come to our rescue."

The divine providence of high altitude winds relaxed for a few hours and we were able to catch up to our flight plan and we landed precisely fifteen minutes after Air Force One. Of course that was expected and nobody from Andrews cared to ask how we had set a new endurance record for one of our heavy back up Gulfstreams. The Air Force One crew hit downtown Seattle and all the shops while we sat on the backup airplane, resting as best possible.

"Congratulations, Major Haskel," I heard from the radio operator's compartment. "You got promoted!"

"Oh yeah," I said, "they announced today. Can you make a call for me?"

In a few moments I was connected to Steve Kowalski at home. I knew it was late, but he usually didn't make it to bed until midnight. "So how'd we do?" I asked.

"Jenkins is on suicide watch," Steve said.

"I thought he made it," I said.

"So did he," Steve said. "Word was nine majors at the 89th got promoted, two of them pilots. Turns out, the other pilot was an officer at the base intel shop. He had been a pilot for a few years when he blew out an eardrum. He still has his wings but he hasn't flown in ten years. Jenkins got passed over just like every other SAM pilot except you."

"He just bought a new car," I said.

"What an idiot," Steve said. "Even if he did get promoted, it takes at least a year to pin on."

And that was certainly true. Each military service is allotted a finite number of officer slots and you can't have a major officially become a lieutenant colonel until an existing lieutenant colonel retires, gets promoted, or dies. I had another year wearing the oak leaves of a major.

The flight home started off as a welcome return to normalcy. We took off fifteen minutes before Air Force One's planned departure time, which they managed to meet. They overtook us somewhere around Nebraska and we settled into the routine of duplicating their descent and approach into Andrews, precisely fifteen minutes later. It was just like the good old days with Timberwolf.

"Air Force One," Andrews Approach Control said, "ten miles from touchdown, you are cleared for the ILS runway zero one left approach." I looked at the time versus my handwritten notes on the approach plate. We were exactly fifteen minutes behind.

"On time," Hank said from the right seat. We were just descending through ten thousand feet, slowing to 250 knots and making the turn to the north towards Andrews. It was just like we had done a hundred times before.

"Air Force One," Andrews Approach Control said, "I show you at the marker, contact tower."

"On time," Hank said again.

"Good evening SAM five hundred," Approach Control greeted us. "Turn left zero four zero, descend to and maintain two-thousand until established, you are cleared for the ILS runway zero one left approach."

"Flaps ten," I ordered. Hank moved the flap handle and we watched as the airspeed decayed toward my next target speed. We were precisely fifteen minutes behind. The next call would come from Air Force One.

"SAM five hundred," Approach Control said, "I show you at the marker, contact tower."

"We need to hold, present position," Hank said.

"Cleared as requested," Approach Control said. "We have no traffic behind you, let us know when you want to continue."

"How's the fuel?" I asked. I knew the answer but confirmation would be nice.

"We can do this for thirty minutes," Hank said. "Maybe forty-five if the weather holds up."

"Yeah," I said. This was highly unusual. Air Force One had been on the ground for fifteen minutes and the President should be long gone by now. We should have heard the helicopter leaving Andrews. We should have gotten the "all clear" signal. We should be landing. We should have more fuel.

"Radio, pilot," I said over the interphone. "Call your buds on Air Force One, use a frequency their pilots don't monitor. Find out what's going on."

"You got it," the radio operator said.

"Hank, are you comfortable landing with less than three thousand pounds?" I asked.

"Not really," he said. "But I suppose we can do that."

That much gas would probably last us 45 minutes, but the fuel gauges weren't that accurate. Our 3,000 pounds might only be 2,000, or less.

"Pilot," the radio operator said, "you aren't going to believe this."

"Try me," I said.

"Pinochle," he said. "Eagle is playing a game of pinochle and everyone is waiting for that."

"That's all I needed to hear," I said. I punched the interphone panel's one button that I wasn't allowed to use.

"Air Force One," I said, "SAM five hundred is bingo."

"SAM Five hundred," I heard the President's pilot's gravely voice. "Your instructions are to hold until further advised and stay off freq."

"Geez!" Hank said. "Nobody calls the man, you know that!" I looked at the fuel gauges. We had 3,000 pounds left. That was the lowest number on an airplane fuel gauge I had ever seen since flying the T-37 trainer.

"Get us clearance to Pax River," I said, "declare an emergency if you have to."

Hank paused, looked at the fuel gauge, and made the radio call. "They are going to have our collective asses before the night is through, Eddie."

"Beats running out of gas," I said.

"Yeah." We headed for Patuxent River Naval Air Station, about forty miles to the southeast. As soon we made the turn the Andrews Tower frequency came to life. "Marine One, cleared for takeoff."

"Get us back to Andrews," I said. "We'll land regardless of an all clear."

"Good plan," Hank said.

We turned north again and were cleared for the approach back into Andrews.

"Contact tower," approach control directed.

"We doing this?" Hank asked.

"Yup," I said. "To hell with them."

"SAM five hundred," Hank called on tower frequency, "marker inbound."

"SAM five hundred," tower said, "winds are calm, you are cleared to land, runway zero one left."

Now everyone on frequency knew we were headed in. If any of the press cars saw us they might have made the connection and our secrecy would be blown. That would hang us for sure. Even if the press was gone, if the President's pilot saw us we would be 89th history.

"I got an idea," Hank said. "Tower, SAM five hundred request a sidestep to the right runway."

"Brilliant," I said.

"Approved as requested, you are now cleared to land zero one right," tower said.

We landed on the east runway, about a mile away from the VIP ramp and perhaps far enough to avoid detection. As we turned off the runway the call finally came over our private radio. "All clear, SAM five hundred, come on in."

"On our way," the radio operator said on the frequency.

"Now you are as guilty as we are," I said, over the interphone.

"I didn't sign up for glider duty, sir," he said. "I'll fly with you any day, Major Haskel."

"That's lieutenant colonel select Haskel to you," Hank said. "And I second the motion."

The next morning I showed up at the squadron, ready to accept whatever punishment was handed out to back up pilots who land prior to the "all clear" and jeopardize the secrecy of the back up program. But nobody seemed to know about it. The only thing out of the ordinary was an order to appear before the wing commander.

"Congratulations, Eddie," he said after returning my salute. "Have a seat."

I picked the middle seat of the three opposite his desk. I only knew General Bullock by reputation and seeing him on the news whenever he escorted the President to his plane. He was a C-130 pilot before becoming a general officer, and seemed content to allow the SAM Mafia to keep the wing's primary mission on track.

"I was happy to see you are a safety school graduate," he said. "We have plenty of those, of course, but not many who make lieutenant colonel. I would like you to take over the wing's safety office. Can you do that for me, Eddie?"

"Yes, sir," I said.

"Really?" he asked. "No push back, no 'but I would rather fly more often,' no extenuating circumstances?"

"Never turn down a combat assignment," I said.

"Well that's just great!" he said. "I look forward to working with you."

Of course it was inevitable. He had to have a lieutenant colonel or a lieutenant colonel select fill the position, and that officer had to be a safety school graduate. The fact he had no choice meant I had no choice. But running a safety program would be a welcome change.

The Lovely Mrs. Haskel was pleased with the promotion in rank and position. "I bet the Mafia is pretty upset that only one pilot out of nine made it," she said. "But everyone had to have known that pilot would have been you."

"I got lucky," I said.

"You made your luck," she said. We were sitting on a park bench near our neighborhood. *Number One Son* was riding his bicycle as far away as possible while keeping within our eyesight. *The Little Princess* was walking from the park's very large sand box with a pail of very wet sand.

"Daddy," she said, "why do you need water for the sand to stick together?"

I took a handful of sand and molded a triangular shape that every child from a Japanese family would recognize.

"Musubi!" she said. It may have been shaped like the rice balls of my youth, but the color and texture were all wrong.

"What happens when you spill a little water on the kitchen counter?" I asked. "Does all of the water go onto the floor or does some of it form little beads on the counter?"

"Beads," she said. "They kinda stand up."

"That's called 'surface tension' and it happens because water is attracted to itself," I said. "Water likes to stick with water so it beads up."

"But this is sand," she said.

"Yes," I said. "Sand hates sand, it likes to fall apart. But when you make sand wet, the water on each grain of sand likes to stick with the water on the next grain of sand."

"And that's why we need water to make sand castles," she said.

"Exactly!" I said. Satisfied, *The Little Princess* returned to her construction project.

"She has such a smart dad," *The Lovely Mrs. Haskel* said.

"Her dad can be pretty stupid sometimes," I said. "But he keeps learning."

"Welcome back, Eddie," she said.

Developing Rules of Fuel

If you know anyone who has flown the same aircraft type for ten years or more, chances are they will have learned a few "Rules of Fuel" that make life easier. If you don't have such an experienced pilot, you can come up with your own. Here's how.

Trip Fuel Burn

Save any flight plans you have where you've flown at least half the airplane's longest expected flight. (i.e., 5 hour flight plans in a G450) Look at the time and the fuel used at top of climb. (i.e., 19 minutes and 2,750 lbs.) Multiply the next leg's fuel flow in pounds per hour (PPH) by the time remaining in the first hour after the climb. (i.e., 41 minutes times 3,070 PPH is 2,100 lbs.) Add the two to arrive at your first hour's fuel burn. (i.e., 4,850 lbs)

Compute the PPH for each of the following hours and determine the rate until the differences hour-to-hour become insignificant. (i.e., 3,010 / 2,810 / 2,730 / 2,650 / 2,550)

Repeat this for a number of similar flight plans and take an average for each hour. You can also try adding heavy weight / light weight variations, or seasonal. The result is a good way to compute the required fuel for any duration flight.

Example: A G450 burns 5,000 lbs. the first hour; then 3,000 lbs. per hour for the next three hours; and then 2,500 lbs. per hour for the rest of the flight.

Altitude versus Winds

The impact of altitude isn't as clear-cut as one might think. Most jet engines do tend to burn more fuel at lower altitudes, but the aircraft's true airspeed increase may offset some of the loss in fuel mileage. If the winds are favorable, you could actually improve your fuel situation.

Your AFM should have cruise altitude charts that provide fuel consumption in terms of nautical air miles per pound (NAM/LB). Pick the highest grossweight that will allow you to cruise at the highest altitude you normally fly. Figure the NAM/LB at this altitude and determine what theoretical TAS is needed at lower altitudes to equal this. The difference between actual and theoretical TAS will be the required wind change to break even.

Example: The normal cruise speed for a G450 is 0.80 Mach which it can do comfortably up to 58,000 lbs grossweight at its maximum altitude of 45,000 feet and that yields 0.1766 NAM/LB. At that rate, it takes 2,600 lbs fuel to fly 459 nm. We can take the NAM/LB at lower altitudes to discern the needed change in winds to equal the loss of fuel efficiency.

Alt	29,000	31,000	33,000	35,000	37,000	39,000	41,000	43,000	45,000
nam/lb	.1234	.1317	.1398	.1482	.1578	.1655	.1705	.1748	.1766
TAS	474	470	465	461	459	459	459	459	459
nam*	321	342	363	385	410	430	443	454	459
wind**	153	128	102	76	49	29	16	5	0

nam* -- nautical air miles for 2,600 lb fuel

wind** -- needed wind change to make up for descent

So in the case of our G450, we learn that fuel mileage does not suffer much from 45,000 to 39,000 feet. But down lower, we need 50 knots of wind to make up for the mileage decrease down to 37,000 feet and 100 knots of wind if we drop down to 33,000 feet.

Speed Impact

Some aircraft flight manuals include all engine cruise charts with various speeds that are useful for comparison. It may be helpful to pick an intermediate weight and altitude and see if any relationship can be found.

Example: The G450 Performance Handbook offers a range of speeds. Selecting a few speeds for 58,000 lbs. grossweight, 35,000 feet altitude, and ISA:

Mach	0.60	0.70	0.75	0.77	0.80	0.83	0.86
nam/lb	.1595	.1578	.1545	.1528	.11482	.1384	.1182
Δt M80	+20 min	+8 min	+4 min	+2 min	0	-2 min	-4 min
PPH	2170	2560	2797	2906	3111	3454	4188
ΔF M80	-218	-210	-128	-108	0	+228	+798

Δt M80 is the time difference from the M0.80 time to fly 461 NAM

ΔF M80 is the fuel difference from the M0.80 fuel to fly 461 NAM

From this we see our G450 gains 2 minutes every hour for every M0.03 increase in speed over M0.80, but the cost in fuel is 228 PPH for the first increment and way up to 798 PPH for the second. Conversely, the aircraft will lose 2 minutes every hour when flying at M0.77, but will save 128 PPH. Slowing down further costs similar increments in time but the changes to fuel savings are not as significant.

Fine Tune Your Numbers

These findings are theoretical, of course. As you accumulate hours in an aircraft you subconsciously log away these "Rules of Fuel" until you have them fine-tuned. You can expedite the process by writing your findings down and comparing the reality with the theory.

[Items in blue are my comments.]

10: Expertise

C-137B on approach, Valkenburg, Holland (Rob Schleiffert)

Andrews Air Force Base started its life in the jet age flying the P-47 Thunderbolt in 1947, the same year the Army Air Forces ceased to exist and the United States Air Force came into being. Its location, just 10 miles southeast of the White House, set its fate in stone. The base was quickly converted to home of one unit after another charged with flying our nation's leadership. Despite this status, Andrews was nothing more than another Military Airlift Command base in the eyes of the Air Force. Money was better spent first on bomber and then fighter bases. The buildings on Andrews Air Force Base, as a result, were usually dated, bordering on shabby.

The 89th Airlift Wing Safety Office building was shabby, bordering on disheveled. It was formerly a bomb shelter and later abandoned to collect dust at first, followed by rats, and followed by a musty, mildewy odor. When I first walked into my new home my first instinct was to execute a military about face and never return. Entering the front door I was greeted by a staff of ten. Five pilots, four civilian safety officers, and a civilian secretary; all looking at me. They were anxious. I stepped inside.

"It's good to be back in safety," I said. "This is my new home." The faces turned my way seemed to collectively relax. A civilian stepped forward.

"Good morning, sir," he said. "I am Mister Charles Foreman, your chief of ground safety. Let me introduce you to your staff and show you your office."

Mister Charles Foreman was a slight man, thin from head to toe with a tightly cropped head of gray hair above a shiny black dome. He spoke with the confidence of a man who had been doing the same thing for decades.

"Forty years," he said. "Thirty of them here at Andrews. I know where all the bodies are buried."

"No bodies," I said. He laughed. My staff included a civilian weapons safety officer, two civilian safety technicians, a civilian secretary, and an Air Force pilot from each aircraft type flown by the 89th. That would be an officer representing the Douglas C-9, the Beechcraft C-12, the Gulfstream C-20, and the Boeing C-137. The Boeing VC-25, the President's Boeing 747, was technically within our grasp, but everyone knew that wasn't actually true. I chatted with everyone for most of the morning. It was lunchtime before I got to the only female in the group, Mrs. Theresa Thatcher.

"I have a number of papers for you to sign," she said. "I arranged them by order of precedence in the conference room. It is imperative that you sign them in order to make things legal for all concerned."

She spoke with a distinct British accent, was about my height, and probably bested me by fifty pounds. She had to be in her fifties, though it was difficult to tell through the pancake of synthetic skin covering her face. She had the natural look of worry formed into her face, even before the slightest emotion was expressed. I followed her to the conference room and found a table covered with paper.

"All this?" I said.

"Yes," she said. "There are many organizations on base that depend on your signature."

"Maybe you can move this into my office and I'll get to it," I said.

"I can't go in there," she said. "Nobody's been in there for a year now."

I sat at the conference table and started at one end and worked my way to the other. In four hours I read, signed, and took notes, over and over again. The staff started to leave around 3 p.m. and by 5 p.m. I had the place to myself. Mister Foreman presented me with my own set of keys. "Don't be too long," he said. "You'll make the rest of us look bad."

"No chance of that," I said. After I heard the door close, I ventured to the room nobody would dare enter, my office. I clicked the light switch and a single bulb from a ceiling fixture came to life. Below the fixture a double wire with exposed metal hung, gently swaying from the air-conditioned air. The desk – my desk – was a filthy wooden creature from the 1950's, standing on three legs and a stack of safety reports. I switched the light off and went home.

I returned the next day with a two-by-four to replace the missing desk leg and a roll of electrical tape to remove the threat of overhead electrocution. After an hour of effort I had a clean desktop but an entire wall lined with safety reports, old magazines, and several years of trash. The room was still filthy, but I had a place to sit. I pulled a foot and a half of safety reports from the stack against the wall and started with the one on top.

The second folder I looked at was topped with a standard "USAF Class A Accident Report" cover, which meant it was serious in terms of lives or dollars or both. The report was stamped with a Department of Defense sticker I had never seen before. The DoD sticker said, "Destroy this report."

The report was of a C-137 Boeing 707 crash in Yokota, Japan, just a few years before. The airplane careened off the runway after one of its engines malfunctioned. Nobody was seriously hurt, but the airplane ended up "knee deep" in mud. The report's photos showed the airplane, sitting on the grassy area between Yokota's runway and taxiway. Three of its four engines were full of dirt and had to be replaced. It was a mess.

Something wasn't right. I pulled the latest copy of the base newspaper, the "Capital Flyer," and read exactly what I thought I remembered: "The 89th Military Airlift Wing celebrates over thirty years and 700,000 hours of accident-free flying."

I called the Air Force Flight Safety Center, which had just moved from California to New Mexico. "We don't have anything showing any mishaps at the 89th," the clerk said. "We must have lost them in the move." It was the perfect cover up. "Destroy this report," meant the 89th safety record was intact. "I guess you can't be less than perfect when you fly the President," I said. The clerk left that uncommented. That was day two on the job.

Leading an office with several safety school graduates, I was looking forward to learning something new and getting to know how real safety officers conduct themselves. In two weeks, theoretically, I should have a handle on things.

I set day number three aside for Captain Doug Weathers, the Boeing flight safety officer. He had the largest program and should have the biggest issues.

We spent all of the morning and much of the afternoon touring the squadron, maintenance hangars, and whatever airplanes they had available to walk through. Doug was very proud of the squadron, the airplane, and the people. He was a good SAM Fox ambassador.

"What worries you?" I asked.

"Worries?" he asked right back.

"Yeah, worries," I said. "What is going to cause the next mishap in one of your Boeings, and is there anything you could have done about it?"

"Let me think about that, sir."

I returned to my office on day number four and was happy to see someone had carted off all the trash, removed the circa-1970 photos from the walls, and had begun the work of giving the room a fresh coat of paint. I spotted one of the safety technicians with a bit of the same color paint on his fingernails and offered to help.

"No way, sir," he said. "Don't worry about it, sir. We got this."

Back at my desk I found a letter from Boeing addressed to the C-137 squadron. It was almost twenty years old. Back in 1972, the 89th asked for permission to fly their C-137Bs five thousand pounds over-weight, based on the fact they needed an extra 5,000 pounds of gas to make most of their flights nonstop. The C-137B is a Boeing 707-100 and is allowed to takeoff up to 258,000 pounds. The 89th also owns C-137Cs, which are Boeing 707-300s. The C-model flies heavier and longer. On either airplane, flying heavier than the published limit is more than the airplane's manufacturer intended. The report was quite graphic.

Sure, you can get away with over-grossing the airplane in the short term. But the damage is insidious and over time the failures to the landing gear system and wing attach points could be catastrophic. Surely the squadron took the warning to heart. I called the Boeing squadron, just to be sure. "Let me speak to any flight engineer."

"What's your gross weight limit on the B-model?" I asked.

"The B model can go up to 263,000 pounds," the engineer said.

"How can that be?" I asked. "Boeing says the 707-100 is limited to 258,000 pounds."

"No sir, we have a waiver. We can fly heavier than the original specifications."

"No," I said. "They turned that waiver down"

"Sir," the engineer pleaded, "if we reduce our B model weights by five thousand pounds, we won't be able to make Washington to Frankfurt, non-stop."

"So what's your point?"

An hour later I found the aeronautical engineer in Seattle who had signed the original letter in 1972. He had moved on to newer Boeings, but remembered the C-137 issue. "No, we never granted a waiver. If you've been doing that all these years it is just a matter of time before your landing gear trunion bolts start to snap. If that happens on landing you could kill someone."

I sat at my desk, looking at my notes and wondered what to do next, wondering what sacred cows I was about to trample. There was a muffled noise at the door.

"Doug," I said, looking up at the door. "Come on in. Do I have you to thank for this piece of history in my hand?"

"Yes, sir," he said. "I didn't expect you to jump on that so fast. You see, every new flight safety officer from our squadron gets that from the outgoing officer with the same instructions."

"Which is?" I asked.

"Which is to finally fix this problem," he said. "But what can a captain do against the entire SAM Fox Mafia?"

"What, indeed," I said. "I've been on the phone to Boeing."

"I know that sir," he said. "And it is already hitting the fan. The squadron commander is furious. If they have to reduce the max weight on the B-model, that airplane can't make Washington to Frankfurt."

"That's why God invented Gander," I said.

"I hope you succeed," he said. "I really do. But this may be one of those battles that can't be won."

"Maybe," I said. "We'll see."

Frankfurt, Germany is exactly where I found myself the next day. It was one of those easy out-and-back trips with a day off for some good German beer and brats. It was my check ride with Lieutenant Colonel Karl Maus as the evaluator. I had flown a training mission with him once, but never since. He kept his mouth shut on the flight over but was starting to loosen up after dinner arrived and the Bier Haus band started to play.

"We might as well get the oral out of the way," he said while assaulting his schnitzel with the side of his fork. I had to sympathize with the pig that gave his life only to be treated this roughly.

"I'm eating," I said.

"We get this done now," he said, "we won't have to take time after we get back."

"I've had two beers," I said, "and you've had three."

"So your advantage, then," he said. "I heard you've been bad mouthing me about that flight we took to Hawaii a year ago. I thought we could take some time to straighten out any misunderstandings."

"Okay," I said, "fair enough."

"So this will be your entire oral," he said. "What is the published fuel balance limitation on the Gee Three and what is the actual limitation?"

"The answer to both questions," I said, "is 2,000 pounds at grossweights up to 55,000 pounds, and 400 pounds when heavier than 60,500 pounds with a linear transition between those weights."

"Ah I see the problem," he said. "You are only half right. Gulfstream publishes the 400 pound limit because they have to write their manuals for the average pilot. But we don't have average pilots at the 89th. We have the advantage of expertise."

"What kind of expertise do we have?"

We have a ton of experience in this squadron and we share our knowledge. From all our experience we've learned that the higher, 2,000-pound limit works all the way up. There is no reason for the variable rate."

"Why is that?" I asked.

"Good question," he said. "You see, at low grossweights, 2,000-pounds is a big percentage of the total weight. At higher grossweights, that same imbalance is actually less on a percentage basis! An engineer like you must appreciate that!"

"Are you an engineer?" I asked.

"Well, no," he said. "But we have expertise on our side. So you see, we didn't do anything unsafe on our trip to Hawaii last year."

I thought about that between bites of schnitzel and rotkraut. The percentage argument didn't make any sense; I had a handful of ailerons on that takeoff! Gulfstream clearly designed the limit with smaller imbalances in mind for larger grossweights. I played with my food some more.

"Listen, Eddie," Karl continued. "I've talked to every Gulfstream examiner I know. I've asked instructors at the training center. I've even talked to a test pilot. They all agree there is no reason for the imbalance limit to decrease with grossweight. We have the experts on our side."

"Well they should publish a flat limit then," I said. "But it still doesn't make sense."

Karl grabbed a passing bar maid. "Where is the bathroom?" he asked. She gave him the international look of failing to understand, the shrug of the shoulders.

"Wo ist die toilette?" I asked.

"Ah, dort drüben," she said, pointing to her right.

"Outside the United States a bathroom is where you take a bath," I said. "You want a toilet."

Karl did a shoulder shrug of his own and walked off. I played with my food some more, thinking about our fuel tanks. The Gulfstream III may have the simplest fuel tank system in aviation. There was a tank in each wing that extended from the wing root outward, almost to the wing tip. With a few slices of my schnitzel I constructed a swept wing and placed each wing tip on a mound of rotkraut. Now it made perfect sense.

Karl returned, eyeing my plate suspiciously.

"Do you know what dihedral means?" I asked.

"Sure," he said. "It is the upward angle of the wing from the fuselage to the tip. Something like what we got on our airplane."

"I read that we have a three degree dihedral," I said. "That's what keeps the fuel running inboard. When your tanks are full, the fuel obviously goes all the way to the wing tips. But the less fuel you have in total, the less fuel you have at the wing tips."

"That's pretty obvious," Karl agreed.

"As a pilot you understand center of gravity along the pitch axis of the airplane," I said.

"Of course," he said.

"The further a weight is from the center of gravity," I continued, "the greater its arm throwing off the airplane's longitudinal stability."

"Yes," he said. "But we're talking about along the wings, that has nothing to do with pitch."

"Well think about the distance of the arm from the center," I said. "If you have a 2,000-pound imbalance close to the fuselage, that is easily handled with ailerons. A 2,000-pound imbalance at the wing tips has a longer arm and will be much harder to deal with."

"Of course," Karl said. "That is also obvious."

"Well a few minutes ago," I said, "you told me that the imbalance limitation should be the same at higher fuel weights." Just then Karl's face betrayed a hint of recognition, a glimmer of knowledge upsetting his preconceived notions. But he quickly recovered.

"No," he said. "I already told you the experts agree it is the other way around."

"It sounds like you need a better class of experts," I said.

Karl dropped the subject and stopped the oral examination. On our return he handed me a "pass" on my check ride with no comments or debrief.

With only two weeks in the job, I was already settling into a recognizable pattern. The first hour of each morning was taken signing memos and reports funneled through the office bureaucracy through Theresa's word processor and onto my desk. The next hour was spent returning phone calls. And from that point forward I was free to roam the base on my appointed duty as the safety conscience of the wing. At least that was what I was hoping for. Returning from Germany, the note on the top of the stack upset the day's plans. "Colonel Paulson, 0700, important."

As shabby as my office was, Colonel Paulson's office was smart. That was the word for it. All the furniture looked to be old, but old in a good way. The bookshelves had good-looking books on them, the pictures on the wall were a mixture of good-looking airplanes and good-looking people shaking Colonel Paulson's hand. The smartest part of his office, however, was the view.

From his window you could see the busiest part of the flight line, the 89th Airlift Wing's red carpet in the foreground with both runways in the distance. Behind the good-looking desk was the good-looking colonel, the same colonel in the bushes I had spotted earlier that year.

"Eddie," he said, "have a seat. I hear good things about you and don't you think for a minute that Paul Paulson didn't have a hand in elevating you to your current position. You are a born chief of safety, Eddie."

"Thank you sir," I said. "The message said this was important."

"You bet it is," he said. "I hear you've been snooping around in other people's business and I thought I would give you a helpful suggestion. You should stick to those Gulfstreams, Eddie."

"As the wing's chief of safety," I said, "every airplane on base is my business. I'm just trying to keep us safe, sir."

"And you do a great job of that," he said. "But just not this particular issue. The wing's been flying the B-model on a waiver for twenty years now, Eddie. You are barking up the wrong tree, wasting your time."

"It is my time," I said. "If I'm wrong, I'm sure that will be apparent soon enough."

"You should drop this," he said.

"Is that an order?" I asked.

"Now you wait a minute, Eddie." Paulson smiled gently, never betraying any anger. "Paul Paulson would never tell you not to do your job. He's just telling you to be careful."

"I will be careful," I said. "Anything else, sir?"

"No," he said. "Thanks for stopping by. Don't be a stranger."

"What's this about you telling the Boeing squadron to stop flying the B-model from here to Frankfurt, non-stop? You know that's going to upset Congress big time if they all of a sudden have to make fuel stops!"

It was my first meeting with General Bullock since he appointed me, though I had been in the job for a month. He rarely acknowledged my presence at his weekly staff meetings and the subject of "safety" was never mentioned. Now I was invited to speak, but waited my turn.

"Paul tells me they got a waiver," he continued. "If Boeing says it's okay, Eddie, who are you to say they are wrong. They are the experts!" He paused. I held my tongue. "Well, what have you got to say?"

"Sir," I said while laying the 1972 Boeing letter on his desk, in front of him. "This is the waiver the squadron points to. The first paragraph is the squadron's request for an extra 5,000-pounds on the C-137B maximum grossweight. The second paragraph is Boeing's denial and the third paragraph is a list of consequences. I called the engineer in charge of the program and he confirms that Boeing has never approved any waiver."

"Congress is going to be pissed," he said. "When Congress gets pissed, the Air Force Chief of Staff gets pissed."

"These airplanes are thirty years old, and we are relying on luck here," I said. "Sir, this got swept under the rug twenty years ago and the officers who started this are long gone and retired. But now it is up to us to do the right thing."

"Let me think about it, Eddie."

Saying "No"

The process of saying "no" to someone above you in what the military calls the "chain of command" can be treacherous, even as a civilian. The result can be an increased respect for your integrity, courage, and abilities as an aviator. Or you may find yourself unemployed. There is no cookie cutter solution, but there are a few paths leading to where you want to go.

Transfer Ownership of the Word "No"

If you can cite a law, regulation, or manual that forbids the intended action, you can effectively transfer ownership of the word "no." It is no longer you saying "no," it is the higher power. Be very careful to phrase this to emphasize your agreement with the law.

Case Study: Low Visibility Takeoff

It was a quiet winter's day in Vancouver, even more so at Vancouver International Airport (CYVR), which was shrouded in dense fog. Alan had already given the company chief executive officer a heads up, "You might as well sleep in; the fog has everyone grounded. I don't think we can hope for enough visibility until 9 a.m. at the earliest." The CEO, anxious to get home showed up early anyway and sat with his staff on the airplane waiting. After the visibility lifted to 600 feet RVR the sound of aircraft engines could be heard across the ramp. "At last!" the staff cheered.

"I'm sorry," Alan said to his passengers, "the airport will only permit air carriers to takeoff with this 600 foot visibility, we need at least 2,600 feet." The staff returned to their seats, dejected, but the CEO stood his ground.

"So you are telling me that if we were at home in Indianapolis," he asked, "we could go?"

"Yes," Alan agreed.

"Well we are a U.S. airplane," the CEO said. "Let's go."

Alan explained that not only could he lose his license for doing so, the company would risk a ban from Canadian airports, where many of their best customers were. The restriction was clearly printed on the Jeppesen airfield diagram and came directly from Transport Canada, their version of our FAA. The CEO agreed they had no choice. Fortunately the fog lifted in another hour and they made it home just a few hours late.

It isn't clear if the CEO really intended his "let's go" directive as an order to his pilot, but many pilots could have interpreted it that way. It may be that the CEO was testing the pilot, to see how firm he was in his convictions. Alan handled the situation well, calmly explaining the restriction was coming from the host country and ignoring it could have implications on the company's business. He effectively transferred ownership of the word "no" to a higher power, the host nation's government.

Pressure on pilots can take many forms and can come from many places. It can come from a senior executive or an impatient staff member. An aircraft owner or family member may coerce a pilot into exceeding personal or regulatory duty limits. A management company, craving that monthly management fee, may push a pilot to go just to keep the owner happy. "Our flight operations manual? Oh, those are just guidelines." If it's a live charter, then thousands, if not tens or hundreds of thousands of dollars are on the line. Pressure can even come from your fellow crewmembers. (Pilots and cabin attendants with "previous engagements" to attend.) Sometimes the push comes in small doses and as each "no" becomes a "yes," the push gets larger.

Delay and Redirect

If you are surprised by a request, a polite request to "think about it" can help delay the eventual "no" to come. "It might be okay," you could say, "but many things in aviation can be complicated and I want to make sure I'm not overlooking anything." If your contemplation still leads you to the word "no," coming up with a "yes" answer to a different question might be sufficient.

Case Study: Seat Time

As a young student pilot dreaming of flying jets, Ben had always considered the Learjet to be a sure signal that a pilot had become an aviator. After years in the trenches he got his dream job flying for a private owner who used his Lear to fly friends and families to one vacation spot after another. Within a year Ben found himself on a first name basis with the owner and many of his passengers. In another year he realized another dream when he was made the chief pilot, running the two-pilot flight department. Right after his promotion, a new friend of the owner started spending more and more time in the cockpit, revealing that he too was a pilot. "What's it like flying a jet?" "Does she land like my Piper?" "I sure would like a chance to fly her!"

At first the boss dropped a few subtle hints, but after Ben politely said he couldn't allow an untrained pilot to land the Learjet, the request became an order. Ben asked for a little time and hashed it over with his co-captain and they both agreed it would be foolish to put a pilot with nothing larger than a PA-28 in his logbook in the seat for landing. The pilots considered their own paths to flying a jet and realized an hour in a full motion simulator might be enough to satisfy the request; it certainly couldn't hurt. FlightSafety International offered a program tailor-made for executives who want to see what it is like flying a business jet and the passenger-pilot readily agreed to the hour in the box. Ben asked the simulator instructor to "be nice," but also to tie in many of the flight events with discussions about Learjet 35 mishaps just to drive home the fact not every airplane flies like a PA-28.

The boss's favorite passenger was thrilled, and humbled, by the experience. "I think I'll pass on flying the real thing," he told the owner. "It really takes some skill to fly a Learjet! I really respect your pilots, Ben knows what he's doing."

Our case study pilot did a good job of delaying his answer and coming up with an alternative that diffused the situation. He also took the precaution of letting his co-captain understand the issues. The owner could have easily made the request to the second pilot and Ben could have very quickly found himself demoted or out of a job. Sometimes the art of saying "no" requires that the person receiving the message believes the person sending the message is sincere.

Prioritize

A "no" answer is often easier to take when the reason behind it is made clear. The very act of taking a hollow aluminum tube into the air seems closer to magic than science for most non-pilots. Sometimes the reasons for some of our decisions can be just as mysterious.

Case Study: The Aircraft Vacuum Cleaner

Chris spent a few years flying for a regional airline with a poor safety record and learned firsthand what happens when corners are cut. He was on the ramp when another of his company's aircraft started engines before getting the "all clear" signal from the ground crew. A mechanic was vacuumed off the ground by the Boeing 737's engines and was lucky to survive, having lost most of his right arm. Chris vowed to never cut corners.

Years later Chris was one of three pilots in a small flight department flying Gulfstreams in the Northeast for a private company with a CEO who was habitually in a rush but usually late to the airplane. One day the CEO called with the orders, "have the right engine started by the time I get there, I want to be off the ground ASAP!"

"We don't do that," Chris explained. "That engine is like a big vacuum cleaner out there and we don't run an engine when there are any people anywhere near it." The CEO protested that the engine was unlikely to lift a person off the ground at idle power. "It doesn't have to, all it takes is one loose piece of clothing to cause millions of dollars of damage."

The CEO, while unhappy, let the subject drop. Chris mentioned the incident to each of his fellow pilots and each agreed to give the same answer. A year later another Gulfstream crashed at the same airport, killing all on board. "They rushed through their safety procedures," the CEO explained to her staff. "I can tell you that our guys never do that," she said proudly. "That's why we hire only the best pilots."

Chris was wise to use the phrase "we don't" as opposed to "we can't." While the latter refusal hints there is room to give, the former says the speaker feels so strongly about it that there is no room for negotiation. Placing the value of the engine as well as the safety of each passenger above the need to hurry telegraphed the necessary message. But this was a case where saying "no" only cost the passenger a minute or two. What about for a case where "yes" has already been given and has become the normal operating procedure?

Play the Safety Card

If all your attempts to say "no" land on deaf ears, it could very well be time to firmly say "no" is your final answer and you are willing to lose your job over it. Another military truism is "don't fall on your sword over every issue, but when you do, make sure it counts."

Case Study: Long Duty Day

Devon was a twenty-year Air Force pilot turned corporate captain flying for a leading technology firm in Houston, Texas. While he never thought of himself as a rigid "by the book" authoritarian, he had always tried to obey the letter and the spirit of the regulations. That's why he was shocked to find out his first civilian flight department was routinely flying 16- to 18-hour duty days in a Challenger

604 from Torino, Italy back to Houston. "Well we used to come home from London in a day," the dispatcher explained, "and that was no problem. Then we got an office in Munich and that put us right at our duty day limits if the winds cooperated. Then we started doing that all the time, no matter the winds. So Torino is only an extra hour. None of the pilots before you have ever complained."

Devon flew the trip, thinking it best to show his "can do" attitude to his fellow pilots. If the other seven pilots could do it, he reasoned, there was no reason he shouldn't be able to. On the day of the long trip back he felt himself nod off somewhere over the Midwest. His head jerked back and startled him back to consciousness. He looked to his left to see the captain sound asleep.

"I agree with you," the chief pilot said when he brought the matter up at the next safety meeting. "But we've been doing this for a year now, if we tell the company we can no longer do this they are going to wonder if we've been doing something unsafe all this time."

After some soul searching, Devon decided it was worth losing his job rather than risk his license and his passenger's safety over something so easily controlled. He let his boss know he would be looking for another job but was willing to stick around as long as needed for any trips that didn't violate company duty rest policies. The chief pilot was shocked, especially when he heard from two more pilots moved to take the same stand. The chief pilot had no choice but to start scheduling crew swaps for the long duty days. To his surprise, nobody at the company headquarters objected.

Begin Again

The best way to avoid these situations in the first place is to establish a no-nonsense reputation that makes it clear to your passengers that you will not compromise your integrity or their safety. If you are in an unfortunate environment where that hasn't been done, it is never too late to begin again.

Case Study: Incremental Waiver

Fred was unhappy to see his name on the schedule for a trip to Hilton Head Island Airport (KHXD) in South Carolina. He knew the company's CEO was an avid golfer and he knew that the rest of his flight department quietly agreed to start operations to the 4,300' runway. Their company rules said their Challenger 604 was restricted from landing with anything less than 5,000', but the chief pilot had waived that. At first the waiver was heavily considered, required optimal weather and a very senior crew. Now, Fred realized, any crew could be assigned *the dreaded trip.*

"I can't run a flight department with special rules for certain captains," the chief pilot said. "Either you can fly every trip or you can't fly any." The chief pilot reluctantly took Fred off the trip and was greeted with a sea of complaints from the other pilots. As it turned out, every line pilot thought the runway was too short. "What am I supposed to do?" the chief pilot wondered.

Coincidently, the flight department underwent an independent safety audit and was presented with a very complimentary draft report. "I didn't write you up for this," the auditor said behind closed doors to the chief pilot, "but your guys are really unhappy about the Hilton Head situation. I really can't blame them; that runway is too short for a Challenger. You might consider going to Savannah instead."

"Could you write us up, please?" the chief pilot said. "You would be doing us a favor."

The auditor immediately recognized the chief pilot's plan and agreed. The flight department started flying to Savannah International Airport (KSAV) for the CEO's golf trips. "We are always looking to improve," the chief pilot told the CEO. "Our recent safety audit revealed we are operating at the highest levels of safety with one exception and we agreed to tackle that exception head on. The risks associated with landing on such a short runway are too high." The CEO only shrugged and said, "Okay. I just want to be safe."

Just as individuals can become complacent and vulnerable to the "we've always done it that way" syndrome, so too can organizations lose focus on what really matters. There are natural opportunities to look at processes from the bottom up, such as after a change in leadership or a large turnover of pilots. Even without these events, however, opportunities can be invented. Each Safety Management System (SMS) audit presents such an opportunity every few years. Flight departments can also run internal audits. Each of these events presents an opportunity to reverse an earlier regretted "yes" into a wiser "no."

[Each case study is true, identities have been changed.]

[Items in blue are my comments]

11: SAM Foxed

C-9C taking off from Istanbul Ataturk (Aktug Ates)

The Air Force bought 21 Douglas DC-9 airliners in the late sixties to fill the role of medical evacuation airlifters and dubbed the airplane the C-9A "Nightingale." In 1976, three more showed up at Andrews Air Force Base called the VC-9C until President Carter ordered the Air Force trim itself of posh airplanes. At that point, the three VIP airplanes became, very simply, C-9C aircraft.

Those three airplanes remained an anachronism during their tenure at Andrews. While all the other jets in the 89th fleet were long range birds with capable communications suites, the C-9C could barely top 3,000 nautical miles and wasn't even equipped with a simple phone. But they were cheap to operate and had lots of seats. I almost never gave any thought to the Douglas airplanes, not even when I saw them on the ramp. But one day, when I spotted one on the ramp with a large pool of hydraulic fluid below its left engine, I became interested. The airplane had just returned from a training mission and the crew was just deplaning.

"We lost the left system," the instructor pilot said, joining me at the tail of the airplane. "It was fortunate that it was during the last approach of the day at Dover, so it was just a matter of limping home."

173

"You flew all the way from Delaware with a failed hydraulic system?" I asked. "Yeah, SAM Fox, you know." That was true. SAM Fox Mafia pilots were fond of citing their exploits against all odds trying to accomplish the mission, even the training mission.

"Did that make anyone nervous?" I asked.

"Not at all," he said. "The two systems are pretty redundant and we lost the left system, the least important of the two."

"What if you lost both systems?" I asked.

"Well then we would have been in a world of hurt," he said. "But we didn't. Hey, aren't you a Gulfstream guy? Why are you so interested?"

"I'm the wing's chief of safety," I said. "I'm interested in everything."

"Maybe this is worth some kind of award?" he asked.

"Maybe," I said. "Did you declare an emergency?"

"Hell no," he said. "You know we don't do that."

"Yeah," I said. "I guess we don't."

Of course he was right. The wing's philosophy was to deal with its problems quietly and avoid any adverse attention that would detract from the stellar record of the 89th. SAM Fox meant hacking the mission no matter the odds, even a failed hydraulic system. There were lots of advantages to declaring an emergency, not the least of which was priority over all other air traffic. But it was something we just didn't do.

I wasn't so sure about his decision to fly from Dover, Delaware back to Andrews with a hydraulic system that had failed. He had no idea why the first system failed. What took out the first system could have taken out his second, and only remaining system. He was an instructor pilot and I was no pilot of any kind when it came to the Douglas aircraft. Perhaps it wasn't so critical.

A week later, I was in the left seat during my own training flight, completing the last of several approaches at McGuire Air Force Base, New Jersey and flying home at 22,000 feet. The flight had gone well and the instructor was chatting casually with the flight engineer. It appeared the "gotcha" portion of the training was over and my only remaining task was to return to Andrews without breaking anything.

Suddenly, whoosh! The cabin air pressure disappeared, the air from my lungs rushed out, it became very cold, and the noise was deafening. I grabbed for my oxygen mask and activated the mask's microphone.

"Everybody okay?" I asked.

"I'm up," the instructor said.

"Me too," the engineer said.

"Engines seem okay," I said. "The airplane is flying okay. Engineer, see if we have a hole anywhere. We're below 25,000 feet, on oxygen, no pax, so we don't have to rush down. Declare an emergency and get clearance for a descent to 10,000 feet."

The engineer hooked his mask to a portable bottle, unstrapped, and left the cockpit. The instructor in the right seat was a bit less dramatic when addressing Washington Center. "Ah center, Venus twenty-one needs a descent to 10,000 feet. We seem to have lost some of our cabin pressure."

"Venus twenty-one," center replied, "cleared for an immediate descent to 10,000 feet. Are you declaring an emergency?"

"Ah negative," he said. "We got this under control."

I eased the airplane down, being careful not to put any additional strain on the aircraft in case we had any structural damage. A loss of pressurization at higher altitudes almost always mandates a rapid descent to get the passengers to an altitude with breathable oxygen. The masks in back were not good enough for sustained operations. Up front our masks allowed us to continue up to 25,000 feet.

"I think we should declare an emergency," I said.

"We don't do that," the instructor said. "You know that."

"I want to put the airplane on the ground as soon as possible," I said. "I don't want to risk any delaying vectors and I don't want to get in line for the approach."

"We'll be okay," he said. "I'm in charge here."

Once we got down to 10,000 feet we removed our masks. The noise level had decreased except for a whistling sound aft of the cockpit. It was cold, but not too bad.

"I think we lost the door seal," the engineer said. "Bayonets look good, as far as I can tell. But I can see daylight between the door and the fuselage. No sign of the seal, I think we dropped it somewhere over Delaware."

The main cabin door was not a "plug" type where inside pressure kept the door closed, it was quite the opposite. The only thing keeping the door in place was the hinge on the bottom and two large pins – called bayonets – on each side and the top. An inflated rubber grommet completed the seal and kept the air inside, well, inside.

We got into line at Andrews, three airplanes in front of us. Our extended vector may have cost us ten minutes, but no more than that. The airplane was completely controllable and we landed. As we taxied in the crew chiefs all pointed to the left side of the airplane. I stopped the airplane and shut down the engines. The lead crew chief pointed to the crew entry door and made an "X" with his forearms.

"Keep the door closed," I said to the engineer. "We might have a problem." The ground crew gestured to the aft baggage door and folded his hands together and then apart, telling us to exit from the baggage compartment. We each made our way aft and carefully exited through the baggage door onto the stepladder the crew chiefs positioned for us. Up front we could see the main entry door's rubber seal, about twenty feet of it, hanging from the top right corner of the door.

"That was headed for the engine," the flight engineer said.

"I'd rather be lucky than good," the instructor said.

"I'd rather be good," I said.

Most of my time as the chief of safety was taken with paperwork and inspections. Once a week I would accompany one of my safety officers on an inspection of parts of the base, many of which were foreign to me. These were usually educational, especially those with Mister Charles Foreman, who remained Mister Foreman to me.

Ordinarily everyone calls the boss by rank and name, or in the case of a civilian, mister or "mizz" and name. The boss, in turn, is allowed to use first names. But Mister Foreman was twenty years older than I was, had been in his job for at least those many years, and seemed to prefer the mister treatment. So that's what I gave him.

"What am I looking at, Mister Foreman?"

"Well let me tell you, sir," he said. We were standing between two brown fuel tanks, both at least twenty feet high and a hundred feet in diameter. At the base of one was a pipe where the brown paint had delaminated. "This here is the telltale sign of premature corrosion and that means we have a microscopic leak."

"How do we know it isn't corrosion from the outside?" I asked.

"Because it is only along the seam," he said. "This needs to be fixed."

Mister Foreman's word carried a lot of weight on base. He could, quite literally, shut down the operation if he found a violation of some federal code or military regulation. Each of the individual safety officers knew their jobs and each of these experiences proved I depended on them to do my job. My pilot safety officers were in a different environment, however. They had two masters, the safety office and their jobs as SAM Fox pilots. Doing the former too well could jeopardize the latter. I was hoping to gain the trust of each pilot safety officer, but each remained reluctant to air any dirty laundry in my direction. When I did find out about an airplane-related safety incident, it was usually the element of chance that clued me in.

The operations group was positioned between the Gulfstream squadron and my safety office and was a good place to take in a view of the flight line and get a sneak preview of the schedule at current operations. Here too I could get a complete summary of where in the world every airplane was and if any of them were experiencing problems a good safety officer should be aware of. As I walked in, the current operations staff was huddled around their command post radio.

"SAM twenty-six thousand has the number four engine shut down with a fire light still on but no other indications of fire." I recognized Lieutenant Colonel Chuck Roberts' voice. "Request you do the following," he continued. "We'll land to the north on the far runway to keep the airplane out of the view of the press. Like to have fire vehicles ready to go but out of sight. We'll pull into VIP spot keeping number four out of view. If fire vehicles see any indication of fire, have them notify us and we'll stop so they can put it out. Otherwise, have them remain out of view until PAX and press are gone."

"Sounds like a good plan," replied the command post controller.

"Colonel Roberts again!" one of the current operations clerks said. "This is exactly the same as two years ago, same airplane, same pilot, same passenger! What are the odds?"

The collective wisdom was that Lieutenant Colonel Roberts was destined for

SAM Fox Superstardom. They might even have to retire his jersey.

I abandoned my afternoon plans and decided to camp out at current operations. We tracked the C-137C's progress into Andrews airspace. The airplane's tail number was 26000, where the first digit was dropped it could have been 62-6000. The aircraft was built in 1962 and quickly became Air Force One for a line of presidents until it was eventually replaced by the Boeing 747. It was an old airplane that still looked new, thanks to the efforts of the 89th to keep it as good looking as the day it was new. But over the years the availability of spare parts inevitably meant more and more excitement. Excitement can be a bad thing with airplanes.

We spotted the airplane to the south, trailing a little black smoke. That was not unusual for these Boeings, their engines were built in the 1950's. They landed, turned 180 degrees on the far runway, and took the long way to the VIP ramp. From our vantage point we could see the fire trucks behind a blast fence, hidden from the press. Once the airplane was nosed in towards us we could see a little discoloration in the right outboard engine cowl but only briefly. The airplane turned right to parallel the passenger terminal and the number four engine was again hidden from our view. More importantly, it was hidden from the press.

In a matter of minutes the passengers and press were gone and the fire trucks surrounded the right side of the airplane. I found my way to the airplane and confirmed with the chief of maintenance that the fire had burnt itself out while in flight and all that was left were the charred remains of what looked like pneumatic ducting wrapped around the engine.

"What are you doing here," I heard from behind me. I turned to face Colonel Paulson.

"I need to determine if this is reportable," I said. "And then I need to make sure we find the cause."

"It isn't reportable," he said, "and the cause is up to the chief of maintenance. You aren't needed here, major."

"It appears to me, sir, that it probably is not reportable," I said. "It looks like a bleed air ducting fire and if that ducting was confined to the engine cowl, it can be considered a single system failure. If that is the case, it is not reportable. But I need to be sure."

"I am sure it is a single system problem," he said. "You are dismissed."

In the end, reporting the incident or not was really up to me. But I could be overruled by the wing commander, the headquarters of Air Force Safety, or just about anyone with an interest in keeping the SAM Fox myth of perfection alive. Most Air Force units long ago decided that anything inside an engine cowl is considered a single system known as the engine. The regulation would back them up.

"Good day, sir," I said.

The next morning I was looking at the same engine, this time in the maintenance hangar and without the crowd. "The bleed air duct let go between these two fittings," the only mechanic present said. "We figure one or both clamps just vibrated loose."

"Were they the right clamps?" I asked. "Were they tightened sufficiently? Do we need to inspect these clamps on all the other airplanes?"

"Above my pay grade, sir," he said. "Can I ask you a question, sir?"

"Sure," I said.

"Why did they fire the pilot?" he asked. "Not much a pilot can do to cause this."

"I don't know," I said.

Fired? Two years ago Roberts was granted SAM Fox hero status for handling the same problem the same way. Now he was fired? The chief of maintenance agreed to check the clamps on all four engines on all seven C-137s. I called the Air Force program manager for Boeing aircraft and he agreed to institute similar checks on all Air Force Boeing 707s. I still didn't know why the clamps vibrated loose. Perhaps we should require more frequent inspections? Perhaps we should redesign the clamps? There were a lot of "perhaps" to consider, but my focus was redirected to my other job. The flying job.

The role of the Chairman of the Joint Chiefs of Staff has changed over the years. The job was created to give the Secretary of Defense a board of advisors for all things military. A four-star general or admiral from each service was picked by the President to be that service's chief of staff. An additional officer was picked from one of the services to be the senior uniformed officer in the entire United States military establishment. What is often misunderstood is that this

179

board had zero command authority; they were completely outside the chain of command. Their only role outside of advising the Secretary of Defense, was to steer their service's training and equipping. All that changed in 1990 when the Chairman of the Joint Chiefs back then, General Colin Powell, decided he wanted the spotlight for the coming war in Iraq. He rushed to step in front of every camera he could find and took credit for a military victory for which he played no role.

General Powell's successor was a low key and modest Army general of Polish descent, something newsworthy to those who care about such things. I found myself in the left seat of a Gulfstream scheduled to fly from Washington, D.C. to New York City, for the new Chairman's first speech to the United Nations. Captain Bobby Fielding sat in the right seat, more worried about the weather than our passenger.

Midlevel clouds and a steady rain obscured the horizon. The winds were picking up and for the first time in memory, the 89th cancelled all training flights. Most of the airplanes were safely tucked away into hangars and we had the ramp to ourselves. The thunderstorms missed the Washington, D.C. area and our only problem on departure would be the runoff from the counterclockwise flow of the low-pressure weather system parked over the Atlantic Ocean to the northeast.

The green Army helicopter appeared just north of I-495, flying very low, skimming the treetops to stay out of the clouds. "He's got some balls," Bobby said, "Only a fool would fly in weather like this."

"You mean like us?" I said.

The helicopter set down right off our nose, in what they call "hover taxi." Today, as usual, they shut down their engines and the Army four-star general strode over to our parked airplane, followed by an Air Force two-star general, carrying two briefcases.

"Expensive luggage boy," I said to myself.

The chairman boarded and headed immediately for the passenger compartment. The Air Force two-star stopped at the cockpit.

"How you gents doing? I'm Dick Reed, the Chairman's aide."

I shook Major General Reed's hand and gave my first of many weather reports. "Sir, we'll be airborne momentarily. New York is looking bad; we might be delayed. We'll keep you informed."

"Thanks," the general patted me on the back, "timing is critical. This is the new Chairman's first time addressing the United Nations. Really important! Keep me informed."

Of course the thought of delay wasn't really in our playbook. We started engines and taxied to runway one left. We had checked a composite radar picture of the east coast hours before, but a lot can happen in a few hours. The picture from our aircraft's radar seemed to confirm what we already knew, we were better off west than north. We took off to the north and turned immediately to the left.

The air traffic arrival corridor into New York City practically begins just north of Washington and fifteen minutes later we were sequenced behind a massive line of airplanes. Bobby managed to sneak us into the middle of the pack – using the "high priority diplomatic mission" story – but we ended up in a holding pattern with another twenty or so airliners. LaGuardia and JFK were both closed; a thunderstorm parked itself neatly between the two.

"What are the LaGuardia winds?" Bobby asked New York Center.

"Winds are at fifty knots gusting to infinity."

"The passengers are complaining," called the flight attendant, "can't you find some smoother air? And, by the way, there's an angry two-star coming your way."

"When are we going to land?" asked Major General Reed.

"Sir," I turned to face the two-star, "the airport is closed for thunderstorms and it looks like it'll be another hour. We're in a holding pattern right now and we've also got a line of about fifteen airplanes in front of us, all trying to land."

"That's unacceptable, the Chairman's going to be addressing the United Nations at 11:30, that's only an hour away."

"Sorry," I apologized, "we'll do our best."

"Sorry don't cut it, major. The chairman will not be happy. You get us there on time, you understand?"

"Yes sir, we will try our best to get in front of the line of airplanes. But if the cell doesn't move off soon, we're not going to be able to get there on time."

"You got shit for brains, boy? I am giving you a direct order to land this airplane now."

"No sir." I paused to measure my words. "I will land as soon as the thunderstorm clears, as soon as the airport opens, and as soon as air traffic control allows me to. I will do my best to accelerate that process. But we may be late."

"I hope you are enjoying your last flight as an Air Force pilot." The general stormed out of the cockpit and slammed the door behind him. Bobby started playing "let's make a deal" with air traffic control and managed to wedge us into the front of the line of airplanes in the holding pattern closest LaGuardia. The airfield, however, was still closed.

The ride was, to say the least, unpleasant. "Did you notice that the two-star is a pilot?" Bobby asked.

"Yeah," I said. "I read his bio last night. He's a typical fighter jock and was actually a fighter wing commander. He ought to know better."

"Heads up!" the flight engineer called.

"Chairman says if you boys can't get us on the ground sooner than 1120, you might as well turn around."

"Okay, sir," I replied, "if we can't make the blocks by 1120, we will return to Andrews."

We landed at 1115 and were in the blocks at 1120.

General Bullock's secretary opened the door and I followed. The general looked up from his desk, smiled, and got up. "Eddie, have a seat." He gestured to the sofa and chairs positioned around a large coffee table. The secretary returned with a tray of coffee. The general busied himself with one spoon of sugar and a two-second pour of cream. I went through the motions of sipping my black coffee while trying to anticipate the reason my presence was requested.

"I got a call from Dick Reed last night," General Bullock said. "He's an arrogant horse's ass, between you and me."

"Yes, sir." I suppressed a grin at the term.

"He asked me to fire you, but agreed with me that what you need is a 'good talkin' to.'" Another long sip of coffee. "So this is me talking to you, Eddie. Good job."

"Thank you, sir."

"Now I wanted to ask you about something else. You heard that I fired Colonel Roberts?"

"Yes, sir."

"I'm hearing that's causing some hard feelings in the squadron. What's your take on all this?"

"Colonel Roberts did the exact same thing two years ago for about the same circumstances," I began. "The previous wing commander treated him like a hero."

"I want your take on this, Eddie. Colonel Edmonds was a fine officer, but he's not here. You are."

"Yes, sir." Another sip of coffee. "There is a mythology about the 89th around our two mottos. The unofficial motto is what the mythology is built around. We promote 'safety, comfort, reliability; in that order.' And that is a good thing. It gives us flying the airplanes three words that guide our every action. It tells our passengers that we have their best interests at heart."

"And that is a good thing," General Bullock said. "I've never heard it put just that way, but it makes me appreciate them even more."

"Yes, sir. I actually heard that, 'in that order,' first from Colonel Roberts. But here's where the problem comes in. We pilots get the '*Experto Crede*' crammed into our heads and we start to believe it."

"Experience matters," General Bullock said. "That's why we hire the best."

"I looked at my logbook the other day," I said. "I have a total of five thousand hours flying airplanes."

"That's a lot," General Bullock said. "I have less than that."

"Do you know what an average airline captain has?" I asked. He shook his head. "Twice or triple that."

"Are they the same quality hours?" He asked.

"Well a lot of those guys are former Air Force. But that's not the point. Do you know how some of us translate '*Experto Crede*,' sir?"

"You mean it's not 'trust one with experience'?"

"That's what it is supposed to be," I said. "It has become, 'trust one who ignores his experience.' We SAM pilots get it into our heads that we can ignore limitations and regulations. We start to believe we know better than the very company that designed and built our airplanes. We become arrogant horse's

183

asses."

Bullock laughed. "Even you, Eddie?"

"Even me, sir. After a while, 'safety, comfort, reliability' becomes 'reliability, reliability, reliability.' When the culture of the organization pushes it, it is awfully hard to resist. I see it every day when the squadrons refuse to obey aircraft limitations, check rides abuse instrument flight restrictions, and crew members refuse to acknowledge wrong doing."

"Roberts was a heavy hitter," Bullock said. "I doubt he can be pressured into doing anything against his wishes."

"I like Colonel Roberts," I said. "But after getting indoctrinated into the 'Experto Crede' mindset, you start to forget whatever integrity you walked in the door with. I'm sure he thought that what he was doing was in the best interest of the Air Force, but I bet he would have made a different decision before he became a SAM pilot."

"So how does a 'safety, comfort, reliability' pilot become 'one who ignores his experience?'"

"When you start to think you are better than everyone else," I said, "and when the system encourages that, it is awfully hard to avoid."

"How many of our pilots are infected?" he asked.

"Infected?" I asked. "That's a good way to describe it. Let me think." The general got up with the coffee pot and walked up just as his secretary walked in with another. He topped off my cup and then his own.

"One of the uninfected pilots described it to me this way. We have three kinds of pilots. First are those on top, the instructors, examiners, and everyone who has made it to Air Force One."

"The SAM Mafia," he said.

"Pretty much," I said. "Well, that's the first group. The second group is everyone else who aspires to join the first group and still has a shot at doing that. The last group is everyone else, those who never tried or were shot down while trying."

"So you're saying it is the first two groups," he said. "They are the backbone of the wing, this is terrible news."

"Not exactly," I said. "I used to think so, but I've come to a different conclusion. You see, sir, I was infected not too long after I showed up. I came with a plan of always holding true to the principles I walked on base with, but after an accelerated upgrade and the best training program in the Air Force, I wavered. We train so hard that we start to realize we are more capable and proficient than at any time in our flying careers. We start to believe the propaganda."

"So what made you change?"

"I noticed a great many of our pilots are only putting on an act. You see, the infected pilots are calling all the shots, so in order to survive you have to play the role when you are on a training flight or a mission with one of them. But when they aren't on the airplane, everything becomes sane again."

"Maybe we have instructors, examiners, and Air Force One crewmembers who are just doing the act too."

"I hope so, sir."

"So how do we fix this?" he asked.

"Well firing Roberts is a good start, as much as I like him," I said. "It sends the message that we don't mess with safety. But he is just a symptom of the infection. The disease is the complacency that comes with expertise. I think we are in a unique period at the 89th. The airlines scooped up our best pilots about ten years ago so those who weren't good enough for the airlines stayed behind and took over."

"And now they run the SAM Mafia," he said.

"It looks that way," I said. "One of the good things about the 'real' Air Force is they have lots of turnover. Nobody gets a chance to get comfortable and they always inject new talent at each level of the pilot pyramid. I think the average time at Andrews for our pilot instructor force must be pretty close to ten years. In most Air Force units you rarely see anyone with five or more years."

"I suppose you've heard we're looking at reducing our average pilot time on station," he said.

"Yes, sir," I said. "And that might be the solution. Trim the tree from the top."

The general slumped in his chair. "Not too quickly though," he said. "You prune too quickly and you might kill the tree." He rose, signaling an end to the meeting.

"Eddie, you've given me a lot to think about." He offered his hand, which I shook. "I'm going to sign that letter you drafted about B-model weight limitations. I'm going to think about time on station limits too. Thanks."

185

A day later the wing directed that all C-137B crews follow the B-model weight limitations in the C-137B flight manual. Later that same day, current operations recut several trip schedules by adding fuel stops as needed for the smaller C-137.

A month later, two weeks before Christmas, General Bullock announced an 89th Airlift Wing pilot Reduction In Force. Ten pilots were served notice that they would be grounded immediately and given two months to find other assignments. If they were retirement eligible they could retire, or they could simply separate from the Air Force. Another ten pilots every four months would be given similar notices until the pilot force was better aligned with Air Force manpower objectives. The wing's hiring process would increase the number of new pilots to compensate.

Declaring an Emergency

The Pilot's Authority

There is a general reluctance to declare an emergency by pilots who believe it is either "less than manly" or will lead to a mountain of paperwork and unforeseen costs. I've yet to receive a bill and the only paperwork I've ever had to fill out was the request for a few paragraphs, in my own words, in accordance with 14 CFR 91.3.

[14 CFR 91.3]

(a) The pilot in command of an aircraft is directly responsible for, and is the final authority as to, the operation of that aircraft.

(b) In an in-flight emergency requiring immediate action, the pilot in command may deviate from any rule of this part to the extent required to meet that emergency.

(c) Each pilot in command who deviates from a rule under paragraph (b) of this section shall, upon the request of the Administrator, send a written report of that deviation to the Administrator.

These simple sentences establish the power and burden of a pilot's command authority. The pilot in command has the power to deviate in an emergency, which is any situation that could jeopardize the safety of the flight. Sometimes exercising that authority is all that is needed to save the day.

While I was flying Boeing 707's for the Air Force in Hawaii we had a pilot land at Honolulu International with a flap failure. The pilot considered but did not declare an emergency. At the last minute, the tower required he land short of an intersection — this was years before LAHSO was invented — or go around for what was sure to be 30 minutes of vectoring. He elected to land and cooked the brakes to the point all eight main gear wheels exploded and they nearly lost the airplane. They had to evacuate on the parallel taxiway, snarling airline traffic for hours. Had he declared an emergency none of that would have happened.

There is a burden placed on the pilot's shoulders as well: emergency authority allows you to deviate from *any* rule, but not *every* rule. You don't want to throw out the entire FAR book out the window.

[Aeronautical Information Manual, ¶ 6-1-1] Pilot Responsibility and Authority

The pilot in command of an aircraft is directly responsible for and is the final authority as to the operation of that aircraft. In an emergency requiring immediate action, the pilot in command may deviate from any rule in 14 CFR Part 91, Subpart A, General, and Subpart B, Flight Rules, to the extent required to meet that emergency.

If the emergency authority of 14 CFR Section 91.3(b) is used to deviate from the provisions of an ATC clearance, the pilot in command must notify ATC as soon as possible and obtain an amended clearance.

Terminology (U.S.) - "Emergency"

If you think the safety of your airplane is in danger unless you are guaranteed everything you need from the rest of the world, you need to declare an emergency. Saying "I have a problem" might do the trick, but it might not. It is better to remove all doubt: "I am declaring an emergency."

[Aeronautical Information Manual, ¶ 6-1-2] Emergency Condition- Request Assistance Immediately

An emergency can be either a distress or urgency condition as defined in the Pilot/Controller Glossary. Pilots do not hesitate to declare an emergency when they are faced with distress conditions such as fire, mechanical failure, or structural damage. However, some are reluctant to report an urgency condition when they encounter situations which may not be immediately perilous, but are potentially catastrophic. An aircraft is in at least an urgency condition the moment the pilot becomes doubtful about position, fuel endurance, weather, or any other condition that could adversely affect flight safety. This is the time to ask for help, not after the situation has developed into a distress condition.

Pilots who become apprehensive for their safety for any reason should request assistance immediately. Ready and willing help is available in the form of radio, radar, direction finding stations and other aircraft. Delay has caused accidents and cost lives. Safety is not a luxury! Take action!

An emergency can be either a DISTRESS or URGENCY condition, as defined in the Pilot/Controller Glossary.

NOTE – A pilot who encounters a DISTRESS condition may declare an emergency by beginning the initial communication with the word MAYDAY, preferably repeated three times. For an URGENCY condition, the word PAN-PAN may be used in the same manner.

Terminology (ICAO) - "MAY DAY, MAY DAY, MAY DAY"

[ICAO Annex 2, App 1, ¶1.1] The following signals, used either together or separately, mean that grave and imminent danger threatens, and immediate assistance is requested:

- a signal made by radiotelegraphy or by any other signalling method consisting of the group SOS (. . . — — — . . . in the Morse Code);

- a radiotelephony distress signal consisting of the spoken word MAYDAY;

- a distress message sent via data link which transmits the intent of the word MAYDAY;

- rockets or shells throwing red lights, fired one at a time at short intervals;

- a parachute flare showing a red light.

The spoken word "Emergency" may or may not have the intended effect when outside the United States. If you want to be sure, "May Day" is what you need to say.

[ICAO Annex 2, App 1, ¶1.2.2] The following signals, used either together or separately, mean that an aircraft has a very urgent message to transmit concerning the safety of a ship, aircraft or other vehicle, or of some person on board or within sight:

- a signal made by radiotelegraphy or by any other signalling method consisting of the group XXX;

- a radiotelephony urgency signal consisting of the spoken words PAN, PAN;

- an urgency message sent via data link which transmits the intent of the words PAN, PAN.

The term "Pan, Pan" is equivalent to saying "Everyone else be quiet, I need the frequency because I've got a problem." There is no equivalent in the United States other than to say something like, "Break, break, I have an urgent message."

Minimum Fuel

What about the term "minimum fuel?" It doesn't carry much weight, but it is a tool at your disposal.

[Aeronautical Information Manual, ¶ 5-5-15]

Advise ATC of your minimum fuel status when your fuel supply has reached a state where, upon reaching destination, you cannot accept any undue delay. Be aware this is not an emergency situation, but merely an advisory that indicates an emergency situation is possible should any undue delay occur. On initial contact the term "minimum fuel" should be used after stating call sign.

We used to think of declaring "min fuel" akin to saying, "I dare you to give me another vector, because if you do, I am going to declare an emergency and that will really muck up your system, won't it!" The term used to carry no weight at all. Over the years, it seems, U.S. ATC controllers have become more empathetic with their counterparts in the air. The only thing they can ask of you if you declare an emergency for fuel is to make a written report of how you got in that situation. You can answer that you had the legally required amount when you took off and the winds and a number of altitude, airspeed, or heading assignments ate up your reserves. That's much better than seeing your engine gauges wind down short of the chocks, isn't it?

[14 CFR 91, Title 14: Aeronautics and Space, General Operating and Flight Rules, Federal Aviation Administration, Department of Transportation]

[Aeronautical Information Manual]

[Air Traffic Organization Policy Order JO 7110.10X, April 3, 2014, U.S. Department of Transportation]

[FAA Pilot/Controller Glossary, 8/22/13]

[ICAO Annex 2 - Rules of the Air, International Standards, Annex 2 to the Convention on International Civil Aviation, July 2005]

[Items in blue are my comments.]

12: Exit Strategy

Spring Snowstorm at Andrews (USAF Photo)

As a "staff pilot," I was allowed to refuse trips without providing an explanation but rarely did so. I was flying so infrequently that I would rather rearrange my non-flying duties to have some kind of chance at remaining proficient. I was hoping to have Christmas at home but the scheduler's pleas and the need to get in the air again convinced me to agree. When I found out I was paired with Steve Kowalski I knew I had made the right decision. Our trip was simply to London and back, but we would converge on the city at the same time two other Gulfstream crews were returning from Eastern Europe.

A dry, powdery snow fell on our wings as we waited for our passengers and Steve worried aloud about the need to de-ice. "She's not sticking," the flight engineer reported.

"I checked too," I said. "The wings are cold and the snow is dry for now."

"Okay," Steve said. "But let's check one more time before engine start."

The temperature was well below freezing. It was too cold for December and almost too cold for snow. Having to de-ice the airplane wasn't a problem, but it would take time and be a waste of money if it wasn't needed. Fortunately our passengers showed up on time, the wings remained clean, and we headed for England.

Since we were a SAM Mafia free crew, Steve and I were able to calmly go about the business of crossing the Atlantic and completing our duties with a minimum of drama. And that gave us time left over for other topics.

"I'm pinning on next month," he said. "I got promoted a year and a half ago, but my line number finally came up."

"A real life lieutenant colonel," I said. "I knew you when you were a captain."

"Any chance I'm going to get RIF'd?" he asked.

"How would I know?" I asked.

"Everyone knows you've got the general's ear," he said. "The whole time on station thing was being debated for months, you spend an hour with him in a secret meeting, and the next day your crusade against the B-model is approved and then the RIF."

"You give me too much credit," I said. "But that is some impressive detective work."

"The SAM Mafia has spies everywhere," he said. "So how about my RIF?"

"I think you are safe," I said. "The first bunch all had nine years-plus time on station. You have less than half that."

"Rats," he said.

"You want out?" I asked.

"Yeah. I'll come up with something else."

It was a common theme we had both seen throughout our Air Force careers. The guys who want desperately to stay, have to leave; the guys who want desperately to leave, have to stay.

Four hours later we were on the ground in London and four hours after that I was in a pub with four other SAM pilots. Steve elected to skip the reunion. As it turns out, I would be drinking with four bona fide SAM Mafia types.

"This RIF is going to cripple SAM Fox," Lieutenant Colonel Shannon said. "You can't have 'Experto Crede' without the 'crede.'"

"I think you mean without the 'experto,'" I said.

"You know what the hell I mean," he said. "You can't replace a lieutenant colonel with six-thousand hours with a captain who has half that time and expect the same results."

"You may end up with a safer pilot," I said.

"How in the hell is that true?" he asked. "You cannot tell me that captain is going to be a better pilot. We are going to start missing block times!"

"That's true," I said.

"Wait a minute," Lieutenant Colonel Newsome said. He had been quiet until now, but I had apparently left him an opening he couldn't resist. "A second ago you said the captain was a better pilot, now you are saying he's going to blow block times. You can't have it both ways."

"I didn't say he was a better pilot," I said. My four adversaries just stared at me, dumbfounded. "I said he was a safer pilot. What happens with a lot of us with all that experience is we start to take chances for the sake of that almighty block time. The younger pilot is not going to perform to the same standards, but he will be less likely to break something or hurt someone."

The four just stared at me, the heretic. "We've never broken anything or hurt anyone," one of them said.

"We had a Class A landing accident in Japan five years ago in a Boeing," I said. "The wing covered it up but I have the accident report. Nobody was seriously hurt but the landing gear collapsed and the damage was several millions of dollars."

"I didn't know that," Newsome said.

"One of their pilots just flew four hours, over land, with an engine on fire," I said. "The fire burned itself out but they overflew several viable runways."

"Was that Roberts?" Shannon asked.

"Yeah," I said. "I like him a lot, but I think he's been corrupted by our SAM Fox mentality."

"Maybe that's a problem with the big birds," Newsome said. "They are getting pretty old."

"We just had a C-9 crew fly from Delaware to Andrews on a training flight with a failed hydraulic system," I said. "A training flight. No block time required."

"One of ours guys?" Newsome asked.

"Yup," I said.

"I didn't know that," Newsome said again.

"We've had a couple of Gulfstream incidents too," I said. "We are all good pilots, no doubt about it. But I think some of us have lost sight of what's important."

"Like your smooth missed approaches?" Shannon asked.

"I am a sinner too," I said. "But I've repented."

The discussion gravitated to football, the American kind. I don't think my hostile audience was in any way convinced, but they were at least cordial. The next day Steve and I pointed our airplane west. Our radio operator was busy with passenger requests and asked Steve to handle the High Frequency radio position reporting duties. Steve relished the opportunity to practice the ancient art of HF communications and kept the crackly radio on, even between position reports.

"What a moron," he said.

"What?" I asked.

"A civilian Gulfstream Three climbed right up to 41,000 feet over Ireland," he said. "Now they are declaring an emergency because they can't hold altitude."

"Amateurs," I said. "How can you make it into a Gulfstream and not know this stuff?" It was a common rookie mistake for some airplane crews, but a rarity in the Gulfstream world. When preparing to cross the North Atlantic, altitude selection could get some pilots into trouble. Getting a climb when over the pond is difficult; so you usually had to settle for the altitude you began the crossing. When you start the crossing you are heavy, but when you end you would rather be higher to save fuel. A common rookie mistake is to think the temperature over land will stay with you over water, it never does. This particular Gulfstream crew picked an altitude over Ireland or Scotland based on the cold air. When the temperature rose over water, their engine performance suffered and the airplane ran out of thrust.

"They didn't know what they didn't know," Steve said.

"There is a lot of that going around," I said.

It was a three-day weekend and the Haskel family's only plan was to spend Sunday at the Air and Space Museum with Kevin Davies. He also had the Martin Luther King holiday weekend off from his normally hectic United Airlines schedule. He was based out of Washington National but commuted from Dallas. Spending the extra day away from home was a bit of a sacrifice and I was looking forward to catching up.

"Rain check," he said over the phone on Friday. "Or maybe I should say 'ice check.' Your part of the east coast is going to be shellacked in the stuff. United is already canceling flights for tomorrow and Sunday."

"They canceled a day in advance?" I asked. "Do they do that often?"

"This is a first for me," he said. "Stay warm."

A pair of intense systems wrapped around a cold front had buried the Midwest and left Chicago paralyzed on Thursday. We got the first part of the one-two punch on Friday. The base was frozen solid under an inch of ice when the day broke on Saturday. After an hour of chipping away at the stuff, my four-wheel drive was free from its tomb and I inched my way to the flight line. I stood on the VIP ramp and looked down at the painted red carpet through the milky layer of ice.

"How about some coffee?" I heard. I turned to see the chief of airfield operations in his truck, the snow chains giving their characteristic "clink, clink" with each wheel revolution. He turned the vehicle so as to offer me the right seat, which I took.

"How does one get rid of this much ice?" I asked.

"One waits for Mother Nature to do her job," he said. "I hear Washington National, Dulles, and Baltimore are all closed. I also heard all our missions are canceled for the next two days, but we are 'officially' still open." He gave the word 'officially' a set of air quotes.

He drove us out to the runway and continued the lesson. "There isn't much sense in doing anything today, so I gave the snow removal crews the day off. We are going to get another dose of this on Monday so we'll see what the sun does today and maybe start to work on what's left on Sunday."

"And then what?"

"Well we got our ways," he said. "A good snow blade or a high-speed broom can do wonders, but not when the ice is this solid. The next step is a good dose of urea."

"Chemicals?" I asked.

"I guess," he said. "It is technically more like a fertilizer, rich in nitrogen. The do-gooders don't like us using it because it harms," more air quotes, "the environment."

"I thought you had torches," I said.

"I can neither confirm nor deny that," he said. After an hour in his truck I thanked him for the tour and he dropped me off at group headquarters. The only car in the parking lot was a blue and white Air Force sedan with an eagle on the license plate and the operations group commander's symbol, 89 OG/CC, the "CC" being Air Force-speak for "commander."

I took the stairs by twos and turned into Colonel Paulson's office. He looked up from a stack of papers. "How's the safety business?" he asked.

"The safest way to fly is to stay on the ground," I said. "It looks like we are doing that."

"I came in to get us in the air again," he said. "But the roads are iced over so nobody can get to the base. So there's no flying to do."

"Lucky for us," I said.

"Anything I can do for you, major?" He asked.

"No sir," I said. "Thank you."

I drove my truck to the safety office but the front door was encased in ice. There was nothing to do but go home and stay warm. When it is well below freezing outside, the inside of a base house never gets truly warm. It was a good night to crawl under a thick blanket.

"Eddie," *The Lovely Mrs. Haskel* said. "Eddie wake up, it's the phone. For you." I took the phone and looked at the clock. It was noon. I had slept till noon.

"Yeah," I said.

"Major Haskel," the voice said. "I just thought you should know the wing is going to launch a C-9 in this crappy weather. They took a blow torch to the runway and carved enough space for the wheels."

"Who is this?" I asked.

"Does it matter?" the voice said and hung up.

I turned the television to the local news station and hopped into the shower. The top story was an earthquake in California, a big one. I stepped out of the bathroom to see the President in a news conference. He promised to send a Federal Emergency Management Agency team to California as soon as possible. FEMA, I knew, was based in Washington, D.C.

From our second story bedroom window I could see a dense blanket of fog and a new coat of shiny ice fusing my truck to the driveway. I pressed three buttons on the television remote and the weather channel confirmed my fears;

the worst ice storm in a decade had shut down the entire east coast.

I picked up the phone and dialed current operations. "This is Major Haskel, what is the status of the C-9 launch?"

"Sir, the airplane is fueled and maintenance has begun their preflight in hangar seven. They will be ready for the crew at 1500."

My next call was to the weather shop.

"We have a 400 foot ceiling, one mile visibility, and severe icing from the surface to eight thousand feet. We expect this condition to remain until 1800 at which time the weather will be greatly improved."

It took me thirty minutes to chip away at the ice on my truck enough to pry open the driver's side door and get it started. I kept thinking about the "greatly improved" forecast. Was it another SAM Fox code? I went back inside to call the National Weather Service.

"All day and night," the forecaster answered. "We don't expect the conditions to improve until tomorrow morning at the earliest. All D.C. area airports are closed."

"Except one," I thought.

"So let me get this straight," I said. "We've got severe icing from the surface to eight thousand feet all over Maryland, Virginia, and the entire Chesapeake. This is going to last until tomorrow."

"Exactly," he said.

In another 30 minutes I was four wheeling to the operations group headquarters. I had the road to myself and lost control once, ending up on a vacant sidewalk. The group commander's outer office was empty so I walked right in. Colonel Paulson was watching TV. "Come on in, Major."

His television was tuned to the weather channel, which showed a red screen with the words "SEVERE WEATHER WARNING" scrolling along the bottom, marquee style.

"Sir," I said, "you can't launch the C-9."

"Well, major," he said, "we'll see about that. The weather shop says it is going to be good enough by 1800. Call them yourself."

I reached across the colonel's desk to his phone and pressed the button marked "WX."

"Good afternoon sergeant," I said. "When do you expect the forecast for severe icing to end?" I listened to a replay of my earlier phone call. "How is it that the National Weather Service is saying tomorrow morning, at the earliest?" There was a pause. Colonel Paulson got up and looked out his window.

"This is Major Donaldson," snapped the voice over the phone. She was the weather shop commander. She spoke at length about the various definitions of 'severe' and 'icing' but in the end agreed that perhaps they had it wrong.

"Very good," I said. "Now I want you to repeat that for Colonel Paulson." I handed the phone to the colonel who took it, still standing. He listened silently. "Understood," he said and hung up.

"Thanks, major," he said. "Let me make one more call."

He picked up the microphone to his office radio and turned up the volume on our wing's common frequency.

"SAM six eight two, this is Ops Group One."

"Go ahead sir, this is six eight two pilot." I recognized Lieutenant Colonel John Vereen's voice, a card-carrying member of the SAM Mafia.

"The weather shop is now saying the severe icing is surface to six thousand," Colonel Paulson continued. "They don't expect it to improve until tomorrow. Can you still launch?"

"Yes, sir," Vereen answered. "We'll handle it."

"Roger, six eight two," Paulson answered. "Let me know if you need anything."

Paulson put the microphone down and looked at me. "The pilot doesn't have a problem with it, why do you? You know this is an awfully important mission. The President was on TV saying he was sending the FEMA team today. The pride and reputation of the 89th is at stake."

"Yes it is," I said. "Launching in severe icing is illegal."

"How do you know that?" he asked. "You've never flown the C-9."

"Give me a minute, sir," I said. "I'll be right back."

I ran down the hall to the standardization and evaluation office. The door was locked. I pulled out my wallet and found my most expendable credit card. Why not? It works in the movies – and it worked on stan/eval. I found Air Force Technical Order 1C-9C-1, the C-9 flight manual. The warning I was looking for was in the same place it was for every Air Force airplane I had ever flown, Section 7: "WARNING: Do not takeoff, land, or fly in forecast or reported severe icing, under any circumstances."

I rushed back to Paulson's office and placed the manual in front of him. "Haskel," he said, "this only applies to the medical birds."

"No sir," I said. "Those are C-9As, this manual is for the C-9C. There was a crash of a DC-9 a few years ago because of an asymmetric stall caused by ice on the wings. The DC-9's wing is particularly susceptible to ice contamination. Takeoff under these conditions is not safe."

"Okay, Major," he said. "I will take your opinion under advisement. You are dismissed. I want you to go home now. That is an order."

I just stood there, speechless. "I work for General Bullock," I said. "I will be calling him."

"Good luck," Paulson said. "He's on vacation in Greece. Dismissed."

I walked back to the standardization office to return the flight manual. On the way I photocopied the warning page. I sat for a few moments and wrote three pages of notes. It didn't seem like enough. I reached for the nearest phone and dialed the wing commander's phone number. It was picked up on the first ring.

"Colonel Thomas," the voice said. He was the 89th Airlift Wing Vice Commander.

"Sir this is Major Haskel, the chief of safety."

"Eddie," he said, "I know who you are. I just got off the phone with Paul. You got your orders."

"Sir," I said. "Let me read the warning to you."

"Damn it, Haskel. Why can't you just salute smartly and shut up? You never know when to quit. We appreciate your concern. We've listened to you. You've had your say. You've done your job. Now let us do ours. What I need you to do now is say 'yes, sir,' hang up the phone, and go home."

"Yes, sir." I hung up the phone and went home.

The lead story on the next morning's news was the FEMA team in California. Nobody mentioned the role of the 89th Airlift Wing or the C-9 and its crew.

Three days later the C-9 was home and I found a reason to drive to Waldorf, Maryland to visit its pilot. Lieutenant Colonel Vereen was a legend in the C-9 squadron for two things: he always hacked the mission and he was always looking for a handout. I called him up and invited him to the local Irish Pub for a pint and a chance to chat, my treat. He quickly accepted.

After a pint or two he started to talk. "They had to tow us to the runway, it was too icy to taxi!" I feigned a look of awe. True SAM Fox pilots love this kind of stuff, I knew. "It took an hour!" This was a classic SAM Fox "There I was" story, reminiscent of the Air Force's Vietnam days. You find yourself in an impossible situation and through sheer guts and determination claw your way out.

"It was still real foggy and there were ice pellets all over the place. We de-iced the airplane three times. As soon as we got done with one de-ice, the ice would start building all over again. We figured we weren't going to win this one. So we asked for one last treatment with a separate truck on each wing. As soon as the trucks pulled away we poured the coals to the engines and took off. You know the windshield wiper post we have? It sits right in front of the pilot's windows and we can see it clearly from our seats in the cockpit. We use it as kind of an ice gauge. Well, it was completely clean after the last de-ice. By the time we got to our decision speed, there was a ball of ice the size of a golf ball on there. I had never seen that much ice on a DC-9!"

Vereen enjoyed telling his story, as do most pilots after cheating death. I throttled my rage and instead kept my face in the "this is fascinating, you aviation god, tell me more!" mode.

"By the time we rotated," he continued, "the ice was the size of a baseball! Center cleared us all the way up to fifteen thousand feet, we had the sky to ourselves. Well, we finally popped out of the weather at four thousand feet and I can't tell you how big the ice ball was, our windows were completely iced over. Yeah, we had the window heat on. You know, that ice never fully sublimated for another hour. When we landed in San Francisco, we still had some ice on the wings. What a day!"

"Have you ever seen that much ice on an airplane?" I asked.

"Only once," he said. "The Herc could take a butt load."

Now I was starting to understand. The C-130 Hercules has a huge, straight wing with a very large stall margin. Perhaps Vereen didn't understand just how the swept wings on the DC-9 would react to an ice build up.

"This is a SAM Fox record," I said. "And I mean that in a bad way."

"Yeah!" Vereen answered, my sarcasm completely lost on him.

I returned to the base and stopped by the weather shop and photocopied every forecast, every chart, every note they had for Monday. I went to the aircraft maintenance squadron and photocopied all the airplane forms. I then drove to the C-9 squadron where I photocopied the mission orders and qualification books on Vereen and his copilot.

I didn't sneak around at all. Every step of the way, I announced to the document guardians, "I'm Major Haskel, the chief of wing safety. I am conducting an investigation into Monday's C-9 mission to California."

I returned to my office about 1800 and found my staff had already left for the day. I stashed all the documents in my top right desk drawer. I considered storing them at home, but shook off my paranoia. "Get real, Haskel, this isn't a spy novel."

The next morning I got a call before I left the house, asking me to see General Bullock sooner than later. I double checked my uniform and pointed my truck to wing headquarters. In the parking lot I saw retired Colonel Edmonds, leaning against his Porsche. He spotted me and gestured me to the empty parking spot, next to his.

"They allow dirty pickup trucks next to those things?" I asked.

"For you," he said, "they make exceptions." He shook my hand and smiled. "Eddie, you are doing God's work."

"How do you mean, sir?"

"You and Bullock are doing a great job righting the ship," he said. "I can see we are on course to weed out the bad actors and pretty soon SAM Fox will be restored to its former self."

"I hope so," I said.

"But you are moving too fast," he said. "Putting a microscope on Monday's flight doesn't help anyone. Give the RIF a chance to take hold and see what happens."

"What should I do?" I asked.

"We have big plans for you," he said. "But you need to take a time out from the 89th. I have some friends at the Pentagon who say they can get you into the number one airlift office. It is the epicenter of all aircraft acquisition and you can put your talents into getting us new airplanes. What do you think?"

"That sounds good, sir," I said. "I think I am ready for a change, but I'm not sure the wing will release me. They were pretty hard up looking for a chief of safety, I don't know how General Bullock will react."

"Give him a chance," Edmonds said.

I left Edmonds and presented myself to General Bullock's secretary, who showed me right in. "Eddie," he said as I entered, "glad you could make it." He pointed to the chairs across his desk and took his seat. I sat.

"I've been fully briefed about your activities following the C-9 flight to California," he said. "I am going to personally take charge of the investigation and I want to thank you for putting a spotlight on this. It's time for you to turn the page to the next chapter of your career."

"What do you suggest?" I asked.

"Well that depends on you," he said. "What have you learned from your experiences at the 89th Airlift Wing?"

"Experience is exactly what I've learned," I said. "I've learned about '*Experto Crede*' and the problems with trusting one's experience."

"How do you mean?" he asked.

"We have a lot of good pilots who use their experience as a guide," I said. "But they are still wary of being fooled by their experience and ready to learn that they might be wrong. But we have some pilots who are so blinded by trusting their own experiences that they have blinders on to outside information. Experience is something to consider, but it isn't worthy of trust in itself."

"So that means '*Experto Crede*' as a motto is flawed?" he asked.

"I think so," I said. "We define it as 'trust one with experience' and that as a concept is flawed. I looked it up the other day. The true Latin interpretation is 'trust the expert.' That may have made sense a thousand years ago or even today in some fields. But not in aviation. We can never take for granted that what we experienced yesterday is still valid today."

"Well that is quite interesting," General Bullock said. "I think you are the right person for what I have in mind for you. We've already started the work of pruning the diseased limbs from our tree of pilots. Now we need someone to get us some new airplanes. I never told you this, but I get calls now and then from the Air Staff with requests for your services."

"Really?"

"Yes," he said. "The top office in the Air Staff would like to offer you an assignment as a program element monitor. Do you know what that is?"

"No, sir."

"Well an element is a unit of budgeting," he said. "The program monitor manages the money spent on the element, in this case, all of the Air Force's VIP airlift, including the 89th. You will be our greatest ally at the Pentagon. What do you think?"

"When do I start?" I asked. Bullock paused, speechless for a moment. It appeared he wasn't ready for that answer but he quickly recovered.

"How about next week?"

"I can do that, sir."

"Great!" he said. "I'll have Colonel Carlson give you a call, he'll be your new boss."

I saluted and left, wondering why I gave in so easily. Was it part of my "Never turn down a combat assignment" philosophy or was I simply giving up on the 89th? The Pentagon was just across the Potomac River so the family wouldn't have to move. After fourteen years flying one airplane after another, flying a desk might not be such a bad thing.

I drove to the safety office. It was still earlier than the normal opening time. I unlocked the front door and flipped on the lights. I walked to my office and threw myself into the chair behind my desk, allowing it to roll away from the desk to the right.

The Lovely Mrs. Haskel's photo looked me in the eye, somehow pleading for me to pay attention. But to what? And why wasn't she facing the center of the desk, as usual? She was looking to the top right desk drawer. Her photo had been moved.

Everything on my usually orderly desktop had been shuffled about. My heart revved into overdrive as I reached for the top desk drawer and pulled.

The photocopies were gone.

You Don't Know What You Don't Know

If you've ever told someone "You don't know what you don't know," they are likely to think, "Yeah, I knew that." The problem is, that in the heat of the moment, we are likely to forget that very concept. It may be helpful to consider the reasons we have to relearn this lesson repeatedly and to study an example or two.

Reason One: The Learning Curve

Like many other professions that require a great deal of training, being a pilot requires a lifetime of learning. Unlike many other professions, the licensing has many tiers. We are often tempted to think our latest license means we have mastered our profession.

Take for example the novice private pilot who works hard and adds instrument, multi-engine, commercial, and instructor ratings. This pilot could be forgiven if thinking he or she now had all it takes to step into a Boeing 737 because the mystery of type ratings hasn't been unveiled. The point here is you can never assume an answer that worked under one set of circumstances will always be correct for others.

Reason Two: The March of Time

The list of "we've always done it that way" things that are no longer acceptable to professional aviation is a long one. And we are adding to the list at an accelerated pace. You can no longer fly to a waypoint intersection using mentally computed fix-to-fix headings, for example. Choosing an IFR altitude is no longer a matter of 2,000-foot intervals below 40,000' and 4,000' above that. How about "position and hold" clearances? Even if you began your aviation career after these changes, you should take heed. Many of the procedures you take for granted today may be outdated (and outlawed) tomorrow.

Reason Three: Geography

One of the reasons so many of our older procedures (such as "Position and hold") are going away is an attempt to harmonize our rules with those of the International Civil Aviation Organization (now "Line up and wait"). The differences are more than cosmetic. Flying what looks exactly like a charted

U.S. FAA procedure turn using the procedures you grew up with in the U.S. can get you violated in some countries. You cannot assume your U.S. training will work when outside the U.S. (Not even in Canada!)

Reason Four: Compartmented Information

Just because you've always done it one way doesn't mean that way holds true for other airplanes or operations. Take, for example, the tried and true "wing low" crosswind landing technique. Some large aircraft mandate landing in a crab because a wing low will scrape an engine pod. Others require a combination method so the crab is "kicked out" at the last moment. With crosswind landings and many other areas of aviation, procedures and techniques do not necessarily carry forward.

[Items in blue are my comments.]

Going Forward

The Pentagon (USAF Photo)

Row 65. I finally found a spot in row 65 of the North parking lot. From there I could see the Washington and Jefferson Memorials across the Potomac and the Pentagon on just the other side of Highway 110. It was 0700 and the parking lot was almost full.

The building, even from this distance, is immense. By the time I got to the highway bridge, the dingy gray facade of the northeast wedge of the five-sided building occupied my entire field of view. I was in a sea of uniforms: Army green, Navy white, and Air Force blue. The building swallowed the marching crowd. With a flash of my identification card and a quick step through an airport-like metal detector, I found myself standing in Floor 1, Ring E, Corridor 8. I hugged the pale, brown walls to avoid being trampled by the hundreds of people going to work, just like I was. Laboratory rats, that's what we were. We were thousands of lab rats in a huge maze, happy to wander the endless halls. No, none of these uniformed rats, as far as I could see, were smiling.

Though I memorized the instructions, I pulled out my handwritten notes. Walk into the corridor until I got to a stairwell on my right. Climb three flights of stairs. Now face the inside of the building and walk in one ring. This will be the D Ring. Now turn left and proceed along the D Ring until passing corridor 10. Room 4D111, five more doors.

A sign on the door said "Headquarters Air Force, Operational Requirements, AF/XORM." This must be the office. No, it looks more like the door to a vault: a black dial with graduated numbers from 0 to 100, an electronic keypad, and a red button. I pressed the button and the door buzzed back at me. I pushed my way in. The sergeant behind the desk looked up. "He's expecting you, right this way, sir."

I followed her through a narrow, desk-lined passageway and walked into an inner office. She closed the door behind me and I faced the colonel sitting behind the desk. "Sir," I saluted, "Major Eddie Haskel reporting for duty."

"A pleasure." Colonel Gary Carlson returned my salute, "a real pleasure to meet you. General Bullock speaks highly of you and so did everyone else I talked to. Please, sit down."

Colonel Carlson paged through my professional officer records. I studied him as he studied my record. He did not make a good first impression. He was short, plump, and wore coke bottle glasses. The jet-black hair hovering over his left ear was combed over to meet the right, covering little more than a fourth of his dome.

"You come highly recommended, I am very impressed with your record. We'll throw you in the frying pan and see how you do. We have another 89th pilot in the office, I think you know him." I nodded. "I've freed him up for a week. I'm giving him a week to train you and I'm giving you a week to learn. Go to it."

My instructor was waiting for me as I left Carlson's office. "You are a PEM," Major Mark Rader began. "That means 'Program Element Monitor.' You control a lot of money, work long hours, brief a lot of important people, and get shot in the face daily."

"So what's the downside?"

"Keep the sense of humor, sir, you'll need it."

"Mark," I said, "we are both majors, no sir is necessary."

"Lesson number one," he said, holding up an index finger. "The Pentagon is very rank conscious and you are not a major, you are a lieutenant colonel-select. Sir." He cracked a wry smile.

We spent the next day on "the books," hundreds of pages of accounts on every airplane I owned. As the Operational Support Airlift PEM, I owned all the airplanes at the 89th Airlift Wing, the DV airlift unit in Germany, another in Hawaii, the C-9 air evacuation planes, and all the Air Force C-21 Learjets spread all over the world.

Our office, XORM, had all the mobility PEMs. Mark was the Strategic Airlift PEM and owned all Air Force C-5s and C-141s. Major Earl "Bubba" Hooper, Arkansas Good ol' Boy and tanker PEM, owned all KC-135 and KC-10 tankers. We also had a Combat Airlift PEM for C-130s and an Acquisition PEM for the brand new C-17.

Mark was incredibly young for a major, but looked older. He made major two years early, and started working twelve-hour days as a captain. Worry lines crossed his pale skin like the fabled canals of the planet Mars. They were hardly noticeable, but they were there. His blond, wiry hair was cut unnaturally short, as if to keep it streamlined to the wind. No doubt about it, Mark had "the look."

Before the day was out I had my first crisis. "I need four million in FY98 dollars," the caller pleaded, "or I'll have to ground two C-135s." It took me ten minutes to find the right books for the Hawaii C-135s and another ten minutes to find the right line.

"According to my books, you already have four million."

"I need another four million." The depot manager in Oklahoma City was making a good case for his fleet. His airplanes were 34-years old and not aging gracefully. Most of the parts were no longer available and that made them expensive.

"How do I get four million?" I asked Rader. "This guy says he'll have to ground airplanes if we don't get him more money."

Mark grabbed the phone out of my hand. "This is Rader, are you bellyaching about the Hawaii C-135s again?" Mark listened for ten seconds, at the most. "The Air Staff position is you can go ahead and ground the airplanes. If you want to fly them, you come up with the money." He slammed the phone down.

"Mark, where's he going to come up with four million dollars?"

"He won't. But at least now he thinks he has to, so he'll cut his costs to the bone. He'll call again in a week and ask for two million. Between now and then I'll show you how to spring that much from the budget."

I had a lot to learn about being a PEM.

After a couple of weeks, I became comfortable with the office routine. I spent most of my time on the phone or in meetings, usually working budget issues.

It really wasn't that hard. The hours were long – from 0630 in the morning until 1800 in the evening – but the day passed quickly. The huge PEM learning curve my office mates warned me about turned out to be just a matter of having some mathematical and computer ability. The day I taught my peers how to set up a formula macro in Microsoft Excel, Mark Rader announced that I had officially become one of the boys.

"The boys," were as sharp as anyone I'd met in the real world. Everyone talked "big picture." At lunch – about the only time everyone in the office sat down as a group – the discussion usually revolved around world events and the status of the mobility fleet. It was more than just attitude. Everyone in the office just looked the part. Washboard stomachs, square shoulders, crisp uniforms. It was an office of Air Force poster children.

The one exception was Major Earl Hooper, Arkansas good ol' boy. While he looked the part, the minute he opened his mouth the first impression was instantly erased.

"You are really lucky, Bubba," Earl said between gulps of soup, "you've done nothing your entire career and now you're at the Air Staff. Not only that, you're at XORM." Today's lunch bunch was just Earl and me. Everyone else was caught up in an airlifters-only budget meeting.

"Me and you, Bubba, we got promoted together, but I'll pin on before you." Our pin-on dates were based purely on how long we had been majors. Earl would pin on a month before me.

"That means I outrank you, Bubba." He looked for me to react. I didn't. Earl was a typical tanker fascist, placing all other Air Force pilots in a lesser category. The fact I was involved with Operational Support Airlift diminished me further. He had a combat role, I didn't.

"The next thing for us is the command list," he continued. "You got to get on that command list, or you'll never be selected for a squadron." Being a squadron commander meant having to baby-sit a bunch of whining pilots and an entirely new focus on life. Everyone in the office seemed to be shooting for command; I kept my contrary wishes secret.

"Not only that," Earl continued, "but you got to be 'tier one' on that list. See, tier one is where all the squadron commanders are picked. Tier two is where they pick the operations officers. Tier three . . . hell, you might as well not be on the list. But don't feel bad if you are tier three. That gets your foot in the door for next year. Since you're just an OSA guy and you just got here, you'll probably be tier three."

After lunch Earl returned to whatever needed doing in the tanker world and I returned to a request for additional funding for a C-137B sitting in a depot maintenance facility in Oklahoma City. Once a Boeing 707 reached 16 years of age, the FAA requires regular inspections to ensure the corrosion and fatigue haven't gotten out of control. Any damage must be repaired, which costs big dollars. All the for-profit airlines had replaced their 707s with newer airplanes rather than pay that bill. It just makes good, economic sense. Of course sanity wasn't a major factor in keeping our C-137s airworthy.

"I'm on your side," I said to the depot's top engineer. "If it were up to me, we would ground the entire fleet. But before I send you another twelve million dollars to keep a single airplane airworthy for two more years, I have to ask you the same question I'm going to get from my part of the Air Force." The twelve million was just for the repairs needed during this inspection; it had nothing to do with fuel, oil, crews, or anything to do with operating the airplanes. We were just fixing them so they could continue to fly legally.

"Why should we comply with the FAA restriction?" I asked, "why not just say we, in the military, don't have to?"

"Because if you don't, somebody is going to die," he said. I wrote those words down and hung them on the wall in front of me. I got on the next morning's red eye to Oklahoma City and repeated the conversation, face-to-face.

The engineer opened a large wooden crate and pulled out a dirty metal plate, three feet long by six inches high, filled with holes and paper-thin from corrosion. "This used to be a half-inch thick. Now look at it. It was the spar beneath the aft cargo door on twenty-seven thousand. All the other door spars looked just like it."

The only C-137 to pass the latest round of aging aircraft inspections was aircraft 27000, the airplane was the youngest of the fleet and went on to fly Johnson, Nixon, Carter, and Reagan. It spent most of its life in a hangar and was babied all of its life. No doubt about it, of all the C-137s, 27000 would be in the best condition.

"What would happen if this part failed in flight?" I asked.

"Remember that United Airlines 747 that lost its cargo door in Hawaii? Or the Aloha Airlines 737 that lost its cabin roof?"

"Yeah."

"Well, those airplanes were brand new compared to your C-137s. If one of these give, and I'm amazed they haven't yet, you'll lose the airplane."

After three days of going through books, looking at parts, and talking to engineers, I decided the bill had to be paid, but there had to be a better solution. Wouldn't Uncle Sam be better off replacing the entire fleet with brand new Boeings?

I returned to Washington, D.C. aboard a Delta Airlines Boeing 757. Stepping onto the airplane I was hit with the "new airplane smell" I often dreamt of. From row 17 I was right over the wing and the takeoff was eerily quiet. The Delta Airlines magazine tucked away in the seat back was filled with everything I expected from these company "ad-zines:" mindless articles about vacationing in spots I'd never see, stories written by famous Hollywood actors with nothing to say, and ads for five-dollar watches promising, "Your Logo Here." On my second pass through the tabloid I found a letter from the Delta CEO to me, the traveling public.

"The airplane you are flying on right now may be leased," he wrote. "We at Delta always place your safety above all else. That's why we are leasing a fleet of brand-new Boeing 757s. These airplanes are complete with all the latest technology designed to keep you safe from takeoff to landing. But it is more than that. We know price is important. That's why leasing this airplane makes so much sense. At only $3.3 million per plane per year, this aircraft is cheaper to operate than the older 727 it replaces. At Delta, safety and economics make for a great combination!"

The Boeing 757 is newer, faster, and quieter than the 707s we still flew at Andrews. They flew farther and on less gas. Delta was leasing nearly four of them for the price we were paying just to maintain one C-137. I walked up to the front of the airplane and asked the first class flight attendant if I could visit the pilots. (Official business, you know. I'm representing the US government.)

The Delta crew was eager to show off their new toy. The cockpit was beautiful, complete with all the newest bells and whistles. We were flying at 33,000 feet and burning less than 5,000 pounds of gas per hour. That's a third of what the C-137 drinks at this speed with half the passengers!

"Who do you fly for?" the Delta captain asked.

"A nonprofit organization," I answered, truthfully.

Sitting at my desk inside the XORM vault, I studied three Excel spreadsheets dedicated to the Andrews C-137 program. The first dealt with operating costs, the second with maintenance, and the third was dedicated to acquisition of a replacement aircraft scheduled to begin in six years. In six years, theoretically, we would start buying replacement aircraft called the "VC-X." Everyone expected that the sooner we got to that sixth year, the sooner the entire program would be "kicked right." That was budget programmer slang for being moved to the right on the spreadsheet, delayed. Budget programmers knew you couldn't mix these types of programs without approval from the Secretary of Defense. He wasn't known for approving such things and the effort was sure to leave the budget programmer's career in tatters. I looked at the handwritten note on my wall, "Because if you don't, somebody is going to die."

I printed the operating, maintenance, and acquisition spreadsheets and started a fourth, calling it "VC-X Lease to Buy." It cost about $15 million per year per plane for the Andrews C-137 fleet. With 7 airplanes, that came to $840 million over the next eight years. I had recently secured an extra $12 million for each airplane to pass FAA Boeing 707 aging aircraft requirements. Of course the first airplane went over-budget by a factor of two. Spread over the fleet, that's $168 million. So the C-137 fleet cost the budget just over $1 billion over the next eight years. And at the end of that period you had a bunch of 45-year old airplanes that were still too noisy to fly anywhere and would need yet another series of aging aircraft inspections.

"You can't mix operating, maintenance, and acquisition money," I heard from behind me in that distinct drawl.

"I know that, Earl," I said. "We VIP types like to break rules."

"You VIP types are a drag on the rest of us," he said. "And for the next month you can call me 'sir,' Bubba."

I spun my chair to see the new rank on Earl's shoulders. I had lost track of the promotion numbers, but knew he would be one month ahead of me. "Congratulations, sir."

"Is the title of that spreadsheet a real program or your personal wish list?" he asked.

"My personal fantasy," I said. "Boeing is willing to do this for only $3.3 million a year. Not only that, we can replace seven old airplanes with six new ones because they spend less time in extended maintenance."

"We got enough work around here without you inventing more of it." Earl found another major to harass and left me to my math. "And don't forget inflation."

I forgot to add inflation? All costs were assumed to go up three percent each year. Boeing was offering a fixed cost lease. It took a day, but the bottom line was a good one.

$Million	1996	1997	1998	1999	2000	2001	2002	2003	Total
Operate	105	109	113	117	121	125	129	133	952
Aging	84	87							171
Total	189	196	113	117	121	125	129	133	1123
VC-X	102	102	102	102	102	102	102	102	816
Savings	87	94	11	15	19	23	27	31	307

I spent two weeks sharing my creation with various parts of the building to rave reviews. The logistics office pointed out the Boeing 757 would need half the fuel of the Boeing 707 for an eight-year savings of $25 million. The personnel folks estimated the savings of eliminating a flight engineer and navigator at $11 million and fewer mechanics added another $45 million benefit. We came out money ahead every year and the total savings would be $388 million. One week later I pinned on my new rank and before that month was out, the first general officer in my part of the Air Staff signed off on VC-X. Things were looking up.

I walked into the office and was greeted by Earl and his wide grin. "Results are coming out today. The rumor patrol says the Phoenix Eagle list has 16 pilots on the tier one list to become squadron commanders, 24 on tier two to become operations officers, and 47 others just to feel good about themselves."

"Don't worry, Bubba," Earl continued. "I heard we both made it, but only one of us made tier one. You'll probably get picked up tier two. I'll be happy to select you as my ops officer."

While I tried to formulate a snappy response I noticed our office secretary hovering behind Earl with a yellow message form. I caught her eye and she handed me the form which read, "Haskel appt SAF Legal, ASAP, re: VC-X," with the ASAP underlined. I grabbed my notes and left Earl without a word. The Secretary of the Air Force was the civilian side of our branch of the military and the civilians called the shots. Their top lawyer carried the weight of an Air Force three-star general.

"We can't do this," the lawyer said. "If one of you fly boys crashes the leased airplane, who is liable? Boeing? Doubtful. But it can't be us."

I presented my case, circling back to the $388 million in savings a few times, but to no avail. VC-X was dead.

"I don't know what to do," I said to Colonel Carlson. "We have rules against assuming the liability on a leased airplane and the manufacturer refuses to assume the liability on an airplane they aren't flying. It's a problem without a solution."

The colonel rocked back in his chair and studied the ceiling for a few seconds. "Every problem has a solution. Get me the phone number of your Boeing contact."

Before the day was out the Boeing sales representative agreed to a face-to-face meeting and before the week was out our office staff and two SAF lawyers were seated opposite two Boeing executives. The Boeing side appeared to want to help but didn't see how they could cede the issue. Our lawyers dug in their heels. Colonel Carlson appeared as defeated as I felt. Everyone on our side of the table appeared resigned to the obvious conclusion except Mark Rader. He looked angry.

"We are on the verge of saving nearly $400 million here and we're being blocked by something that really doesn't matter!" His venom was aimed at both sides of the table.

"It doesn't matter to you, major," one of the SAF lawyers said, "but this program is going nowhere because it matters to us."

"If we crash an airplane," Mark said, "everyone is liable. It doesn't matter what the contract says, you know damned well we're all going to be sued."

Everyone started talking at once. "Hold on," Carlson said, raising both hands. "Finish your thought, Mark."

"You guys," he said pointing a finger to the Boeing executives, "you guys have the deepest pockets and no matter what the lease says, you are going to court.

You know that." The execs nodded their heads. "You stand to make a lot of money here and we stand to save a lot of money. In the end, this is good for Boeing, the Air Force, and the American taxpayer. You might as well suck it up and assume the liability."

"I see your point," one of the Boeing executives said. "Let me take this back to Seattle." Nothing, of course, could be settled without their chief executive officer's okay.

"Where's Earl?" His jacket was missing from the coat rack and his computer was shut off. "It's only 5 p.m. How can he be gone an hour early?"

"He was kind of upset," Mark Rader said. "He found out he was tier three on the Phoenix Eagle list. Said 'to hell with it' and left." He handed me a stapled list with the words "1995 Phoenix Eagles" plastered on top. The first page was titled "Tier One" in bold print followed by 16 names, in alphabetical order. Number 7 on the list was mine. "You never saw this," he said. The tiered list was secret, available only to General officers making command selections. Everyone else only saw one list with all 87 names in alphabetical order. "You're going to be a squadron commander."

"I don't want to be a commander," I complained that night to *The Lovely Mrs. Haskell.*

"Sure you do," she said. "This will give you a chance to apply all your negative experiences in a positive way. You always say 'I learned from the worst.' Now you can prove that."

A month later I was offered command of the VIP unit in Germany, flying 9 Learjets, 3 Gulfstreams, and a Boeing 737. It was a squadron of 90 officers, 40 enlisted personnel, and 10 civilians. Their current commander was being dismissed after being charged with 13 counts of misconduct. The squadron was undermanned, morale was low, and the workload was high. A month after that, I left the Pentagon for the last time.

Row 65. I purposely parked in row 65 of the north parking lot. Leaving the eighth corridor of the Pentagon toward the Highway 110 overpass gave you a great view of the Washington Monument as you walked toward the Potomac. It was ten in the morning and I had the path to myself. Everyone was inside, hard at work. It must be terrible to work at the Pentagon. Like I used to.

"Eddie! Eddie!" I turned around and saw Major Mark Rader. "Eddie, stop. We just found out. The Secretary of Defense just approved VC-X."

"Wow," I said. "I guess sanity isn't as rare as they say."

"Everyone is talking about you like you are some kind of rock star," Mark went on. "You came up with a new program, rammed it through the system, got selected for command, and left. Only bad thing is the program got approved the day after your official departure, so you won't get official credit for it."

"Official credit is for official chumps," I said. "You can get a lot more done if you don't worry about credit." I resumed my walk and Mark followed.

"Colonel Carlson wanted me to ask you about one last favor."

"Sure," I said. "I'm on a flight to Germany in three days, so it has to be quick."

"We were talking about how to do an Air Staff tour on steroids," Mark said. "Colonel Carlson said you seem to have a gift for soaking up experience and moving on with the needed lessons. He was hoping you would write us a paragraph or two about the concept of experience."

I thought about it as we walked. *Experto Crede,* the thought still haunted me. While few pilots know much Latin, Mark and I would trade phrases now and then.

"You know what *'experto crede'* means, Mark?"

"Of course. Trust one with experience. That gets pounded into every SAM Fox pilot."

"That's what the 89th says it means," I said. "But the true Latin translation is 'trust the expert.'"

Mark raised an eyebrow. "Experience does not make the expert."

"Exactly," I said. "As pilots, as officers, as human beings, we all learn from our experiences and that is good. But we don't always learn the right things. When we cut a few corners in the cockpit and get from Point A to Point B a little faster using a little less gas, we might learn that cutting corners is smart, but the right lesson might be that sometimes we get lucky."

"We've all been there," he said.

"Yes, we have." My thoughts formed slowly. It was a concept I felt, but had never articulated. "We are all terrible judges of cause and effect. When we get away with something, our subconscious files that away. The first time we feel a little guilty that we violated a rule, regulation, or just some idea that we used to hold dear. The second time it gets a little easier. After a while we accept all the rule bending as okay. *Exitus acta probat.* The result justifies the deeds."

"Ah," he said. "The 'smooth missed approach' as the prime example."

"Yeah," I said, "but it doesn't have to be something that flagrant. In fact, playing it safe can produce a negative lesson too."

"Sure, but what about us guys flying desks?"

"Remember the push back we got with VC-X?" I asked. "We were told by everyone in the building we couldn't mix operational, maintenance, and acquisition money. They learned that lesson from experience. But as a new guy I didn't let that stop me. Then the lawyers chimed in, and I pretty much caved. In my life experience, you can't beat a lawyer citing liability. That's when you broke with all past experience and shocked us all into a new way of thinking about things."

We reached my truck and Mark stood silently, his back to the Pentagon, facing me. He was waiting for more.

"The math comes easy," I said. "Its concrete, irrefutable laws do not bend. We can depend on its unwavering reliability and repeatability. But flying is more than math; it is judgment and decision making. It requires we listen to our experiences, but apply all the knowledge that goes with it. We, who are experienced, are at risk of ignoring that knowledge because we are blinded by our experiences."

"We pilots need another motto," he said. "Experience is a good thing, but the truth is more important."

The synapses finally fired.

"*Carpe veritas*," I said. "Seek truth."

"*Ita disimus omnes*," Mark said. "So say we all."

Postscript

In a career of collecting flight lessons, this one was perhaps the most difficult. Let me explain why.

The men and women of the 89th Airlift Wing are among the finest aviators I have ever had the privilege of being associated with. I am very proud of my Special Air Missions heritage and being a member of SAM Fox. The wing hires only the finest, trains extremely hard, and spares no expense at ensuring all of its crewmembers are highly proficient.

If you take someone who is very good at something and give them all the tools to excel, they can start to believe they are better than they really are. Among some of our pilots, the wing's unofficial motto, "Safety, Comfort, Reliability" became "Reliability, Reliability, Reliability."

We used to joke that these pilots made up a SAM Mafia because while I was there they were running the show; if you ever crossed them, you would find yourself outside looking in. But it wasn't so much of a crime family as it was a disease. It took over your very way of thinking. "We are so good, we don't have to follow the rules."

I tried to learn all that I could while holding to my secret plan to change the system from within. Along the way I became infected. I joined the SAM Mafia.

It took me a year to realize that most SAM pilots were play acting for the SAM Mafia because they had to. These pilots only knelt to the SAM Mafia when in their presence. Left alone, they secretly kept true to "Safety, Comfort, Reliability." I elected to confront the SAM Mafia directly and, with some help, started a change that I hope had a lasting impact.

Along the way I learned that I, perhaps more than most, need to continually remind myself of one thing:

It is better to learn from experience than to rely on it.

References

14 CFR 25, Title 14: Aeronautics and Space, Airworthiness Standards: Transport Category Airplanes, Federal Aviation Administration, Department of Transportation

14 CFR 91, Title 14: Aeronautics and Space, General Operating and Flight Rules, Federal Aviation Administration, Department of Transportation

14 CFR 135, Title 14: Aeronautics and Space, Operating Requirements: Commuter and On Demand Operations and Rules Governing Persons on Board Such Aircraft, Federal Aviation Administration, Department of Transportation

Aeronautical Information Manual, U.S. Department of Transportation

Air Traffic Organization Policy Order JO 7110.10X, April 3, 2014, U.S. Department of Transportation

Didier, Chris, Lieutenant Colonel, USAF – Retired F-15E Instructor Pilot, interview 6 August 2016

FAA Order 8900

FAA Pilot/Controller Glossary, 8/22/13

Huntzinger, David, Ph.D., "In the PINC," Business & Commercial Aviation, January 2006

ICAO Annex 2 - Rules of the Air, International Standards, Annex 2 to the Convention on International Civil Aviation, July 2005

ICAO Annex 6 - Operation of Aircraft - Part 1 Commercial Aircraft, International Standards and Recommended Practices, Annex 6 to the Convention on International Civil Aviation, Part I, July 2010

ICAO Annex 6 - Operation of Aircraft - Part 2 General Aviation, International Standards and Recommended Practices, Annex 6 to the Convention on International Civil Aviation, Part II, July 2008

Report to the Presidential Commission on the Space Shuttle Challenger Accident, June 6th, 1986, Washington, D.C.

Vaughn, Dianne, The Challenger Launch Decision: Risky Technology, Culture, and Deviance at NASA, The University of Chicago Press, Chicago and London, 1996.

www.dictionary.com

Index of Flight Lessons

About the Author

James Albright is an average pilot with average stick and rudder skills, but has an above average desire to learn and instruct. He spent twenty years in the United States Air Force as an aircraft commander, instructor pilot, evaluator pilot, and squadron commander. After retiring as a lieutenant colonel, he went on to fly for several private and commercial operators as an international captain, check airman, and chief pilot. His logbook includes the T-37B, T-38A, KC-135A, Boeing 707, Boeing 747, Challenger 604, and the Gulfstream III, IV, V, and 450.

His website, www.code7700.com attracts over a million hits each month and his articles have appeared in several magazines, most notably Business & Commercial Aviation.

While he claims to be devoid of ego, that can hardly be true of someone willing to write a five volume set of flight lessons based on his own experiences.